Palgrave Macmillan Studies in Banking and Financial Institutions

Series Editor: **Professor Philip Molyneux**

The Palgrave Macmillan Studies in Banking and Financial Institutions are international in orientation and include studies of banking within particular countries or regions, and studies of particular themes such as Corporate Banking, Risk Management, Mergers and Acquisitions, etc. The books are focused upon research and practice, and include up-to-date and innovative studies on contemporary topics in banking that have global impact and influence.

Titles include:

Yener Altunbas, Blaise Gadanecz and Alper Kara
SYNDICATED LOANS
A Hybrid of Relationship Lending and Publicly Traded Debt

Elena Beccalli
IT AND EUROPEAN BANK PERFORMANCE

Santiago Carbó, Edward P.M. Gardener and Philip Molyneux
FINANCIAL EXCLUSION

Allessandro Carretta, Franco Fiordelisi and Gianluca Mattarocci (*editors*)
NEW DRIVERS OF PERFORMANCE IN A CHANGING WORLD

Violaine Cousin
BANKING IN CHINA

Franco Fiordelisi and Philip Molyneux
SHAREHOLDER VALUE IN BANKING

Hans Gensberg and Cho-Hoi Hui
THE BANKING CENTRE IN HONG KONG
Competition, Efficiency, Performance and Risk

Munawar Iqbal and Philip Molyneux
THIRTY YEARS OF ISLAMIC BANKING
History, Performance and Prospects

Kimio Kase and Tanguy Jacopin
CEOs AS LEADERS AND STRATEGY DESIGNERS
Explaining the Success of Spanish Banks

M. Mansoor Khan and M. Ishaq Bhatti
DEVELOPMENTS IN ISLAMIC BANKING
The Case of Pakistan

Mario La Torre and Gianfranco A. Vento
MICROFINANCE

Philip Molyneux and Munawar Iqbal
BANKING AND FINANCIAL SYSTEMS IN THE ARAB WORLD

Philip Molyneux and Eleuterio Vallelado (*editors*)
FRONTIERS OF BANKS IN A GLOBAL WORLD

Anastasia Nesvetailova
FRAGILE FINANCE
Debt, Speculation and Crisis in the Age of Global Credit

Andrea Schertler
THE VENTURE CAPITAL INDUSTRY IN EUROPE

Alfred Slager
THE INTERNATIONALIZATION OF BANKS

Noël K. Tshiani
BUILDING CREDIBLE CENTRAL BANKS
Policy Lessons for Emerging Economies

Palgrave Macmillan Studies in Banking and Financial Institutions
Series Standing Order ISBN 1–4039–4872–0

You can receive future titles in this series as they are published by placing a standing order. Please contact your bookseller or, in case of difficulty, write to us at the address below with your name and address, the title of the series and one of the ISBNs quoted above.

Customer Services Department, Macmillan Distribution Ltd, Houndmills, Basingstoke, Hampshire RG21 6XS, England

---

Also by Dr Noël K. Tshiani

Vision Pour Une Monnaie Forte (Paris 2008)

The views expressed in this book are those of the author only, and cannot be attributed to any institution or current employer.

Building Credible Central Banks

Policy Lessons for Emerging Economies

Noël K. Tshiani

palgrave
macmillan

First published 2008 by
PALGRAVE MACMILLAN
Houndmills, Basingstoke, Hampshire RG21 6XS and
175 Fifth Avenue, New York, N.Y. 10010
Companies and representatives throughout the world

PALGRAVE MACMILLAN is the global academic imprint of the Palgrave Macmillan division of St. Martin's Press, LLC and of Palgrave Macmillan Ltd. Macmillan® is a registered trademark in the United States, United Kingdom and other countries. Palgrave is a registered trademark in the European Union and other countries.

ISBN-13: 978–0–230–21882–6 hardback
ISBN-10: 0–230–21882–2 hardback

This book is printed on paper suitable for recycling and made from fully managed and sustained forest sources. Logging, pulping and manufacturing processes are expected to conform to the environmental regulations of the country of origin.

A catalogue record for this book is available from the British Library.

A catalog record for this book is available from the Library of Congress.

10 9 8 7 6 5 4 3 2 1
17 16 15 14 13 12 11 10 09 08

Printed and bound in Great Britain by
CPI Antony Rowe, Chippenham and Eastbourne

In loving memory of:
Emerence,
Rosalie and
Damas

To all of my country men and women who have been the silent victims of hyperinflation. They deserve to have a strong currency and a powerful and credible central bank.

To my wife Marie Louise for her love and support, and our children Noel Jr, Patrick, Joel and Daniel

Contents

Foreword

It is a distinct pleasure to write a Foreword to Dr Noël K. Tshiani's important book, *Building Credible Central Banks: Policy Lessons for Emerging Economies*. Dr Tshiani's ultimate goal is the restoration of his native Democratic Republic of the Congo to a robust and sustainable economic growth path. He believes that the recent democratic elections have provided the necessary political window of opportunity for his proposed strategic agenda.

The prerequisite for the success of this mission, he is convinced, is the development of a sophisticated and well-regulated financial system that is underpinned by monetary stability and characterized by a sound currency that, reciprocally, lends credibility to the central bank. He also sees a credible central bank as critical to the promotion and efficient regulation of any modern financial system. Indeed, the author dreams of the day when his country's money is a key currency within Africa, and Kinshasa a major world financial centre. But everything is contingent upon an environment of responsible fiscal policy and a strong political commitment to the reform process.

Dr Tshiani's education, training and experience give him a fighting chance of achieving his goal. He holds a PhD in Economics from the University of Paris IX–Dauphine with specialization in Banking and Finance, and Masters degrees in Business Administration and Economics from Adelphi University in New York, and the University of Liège in Belgium, with concentration in Banking, Finance and Capital Markets. He has also had extensive and varied hands-on experience relevant to the exercise he has undertaken. Sixteen years at the World Bank, including a stint as Resident Bank Representative in Chad, decades of involvement in international banking, financial and development related issues, as well in developmental exercises in his own country – especially in respect of the Central Bank of the Congo – have made him adept at marrying theory with practice.

I must disclose a deep empathy with the author. When Barbados withdrew from the Eastern Caribbean Currency Authority in 1972, I was appointed founding Governor of the Central Bank of Barbados at the tender age of 39. I held this position until 1987. My mandate then was essentially the same as that which Dr Tshiani recommends for the emerging economies: establishment of a 'credible' central bank, maintenance of a stable monetary regime, and development of efficient capital markets.

In July 1975, the Barbados government, on my advice, pegged the Barbadian dollar to the US currency at the rate of $BDS 2.00 = $US 1.00. This represented an upward revaluation of nearly 10 per cent, raising eyebrows at the International Monetary Fund and the World Bank. Indeed, there was no time during my term of office that the IMF and World Bank did not consider the Barbadian currency to be overvalued; yet its value in relation to the US dollar remains the same to this day.

My philosophy of central banking was then, and remains, very similar to that of the author. We both take seriously John Maynard Keynes's famous dictum that the most certain way to undermine a society is to 'debauch the currency' and so we consider a sound currency crucial to sustainable economic growth; we both reject the 'one-size-fits-all' programmes traditionally pushed on developing countries by multinational financial organizations; we both insist upon the exclusion of political considerations from central banking operations; and we both stress the importance of a sophisticated financial system to the implementation of monetary policy. Central banks expand or contract economic activity by, respectively, buying or selling financial securities in capital markets; such so-called 'open market' operations cannot be efficiently carried out in a primitive financial system. Indeed, the Central Bank of Barbados took the lead in promoting the development of money and capital markets, the establishment of a Stock Exchange and the promotion of the island as an offshore financial centre that today makes a substantial contribution to national gross domestic product.

The Central Bank of Barbados has always enjoyed operational autonomy, but never independence to the extent that the author proposes. However, since leaving the Bank I have, in my book, *Central Banking in Theory and Practice: a Small State Perspective*, strongly advocated enhanced institutional freedom for Caribbean central banks, some of which had functioned at times as mere printing presses of currency to finance runaway government deficits. I strongly support Dr Tshiani's uncompromising position on the issue of central bank independence and accountability.

Following an Executive Summary, a Preface and a brief Introduction, Dr Tshiani sets out in Chapter 1 the quintessential elements of a central banking model relevant to the political, cultural and economic realities of the Democratic Republic of the Congo. First is the assignment of clear and realistic goals to the central bank. At the top of the list is an acceptable rate of inflation, whether explicit or implicit. He does not exclude employment and economic growth as legitimate goals, 'provided there is a clear understanding that there can be no central bank target for the level of employment or the rate of growth in gross domestic product', since several non-economic factors impinge on those two outcomes, which are beyond the influence of the central bank and often of government. Second is the imperative of central bank independence. Third is the need for transparency in central banking operations, and persuasion of the broad public that price stability is critical to sustainable economic development. This educational process will take several years, so the quicker it begins, the better.

The corresponding challenge for the Central Bank of Barbados was to persuade the public at large of the toxic relationship between excessive across-the-board wage increases and exchange rate stability, an argument which I kept before the public for more than a decade in the face of vigorous trade union opposition. Less than five years after my departure the same trade unions accepted an 8 per cent wage reduction to preclude the currency devaluation demanded by the International Monetary Fund.

In Chapter 2, the author makes his case for an independent Central Bank of the Congo. Until recently the Central Bank of the Congo operated in almost total submission to government, resulting in calamitous high rates of inflation and poor economic performance. Dr Tshiani believes, as I do, that central bank independence is a necessary, though not sufficient, requirement for the Congo's escape from its high inflationary past.

Noting the recent trend towards the ceding by governments of increasing independence to central banks, e.g. the Bank of England, Dr Tshiani presents a most scholarly, exhaustive and informative historical survey of the degree and implications of independence enjoyed by leading central banks, and finds the European Central Bank and the United States Federal Reserve System to be the most attractive models. In an Appendix, he pays his greatest tribute to the former Bundesbank, seeing the European Central Bank as its virtual offspring.

Dr Tshiani sees the current interregnum in the governance of the Central Bank of the Congo to be an appropriate occasion for launching his initiative for building a 'credible' central bank and a modern financial system in his country. Drawing on the lessons from theoretical and empirical analysis in the earlier chapters, he sets out in great detail the strategic institutional, organizational and policy- and decision-making processes to be brought into existence. By 'strategic', we mean the critical areas where hard decisions must be taken today if the desired goals are to be achieved tomorrow. Such strategic decisions, Dr Tshiani believes, have to be taken in the areas of: (i) central bank independence, involving relationships between the executive, Parliament and governor of the Central Bank of the Congo; (ii) communications, involving transparency of central bank decision-making processes, and educational outreach to the citizenry; (iii) reform of central bank policy and decision-making processes to accommodate the special political, economic and cultural characteristics of the Democratic Republic of the Congo; (iv) establishment of a deposit insurance scheme; (v) financial sector reform; and (vi) currency reform.

Dr Tshiani has no doubts about the enormity of the challenge he poses for his country men and women. He knows, for example, that the success of a regime of central bank independence depends on the chemistry between the president of the country and the governor of the central bank and, indeed, on the personal skills of the numerous players involved, including the prime minister, the minister of finance and the legislators. Even a reformed Central Bank of the Congo will never be perfect, but it is the only game in town. If it can wean the economy of the Congo away from its habitual inflationary ways and take it some distance along the road to price stability and better functioning financial markets, Dr Tshiani's efforts will have been worthwhile. His book should be required reading for students of central banking everywhere, for staff members of central banks and ministers of finance and their staffs as well as for legislators, especially in developing countries afflicted by high inflation and collapsing currencies, and especially for interested laymen in the Democratic Republic of the Congo.

Sir Courtney N. Blackman, PhD
Founding Governor of the Central Bank of Barbados,
Former Ambassador to the USA and the
Organization of American States,
Author of: *Central Banking in Theory and Practice* (1995)
and *The Practice of Economic Management* (2006)

Executive Summary

Imagine a country with a total land size of 2,342,000 square kilometres, a population of 62 million people and abundant natural resources (diamond, copper, cobalt, uranium, magnesium, coltan, phosphate, petroleum, oil, agricultural products, woods, timber, coffee, cocao, etc.), but with the whole of the banking sector having only 778 million dollars in assets, 50,000 bank accounts, and the largest of the eleven banks in the country with only 185 million dollars in assets, and 51 million in loans! Imagine that, out of 62 million people, only 0.5 per cent of them has access to any kind of financial services. Imagine that in this country, one cannot get a mortgage to buy a home, nor a small loan to start a small business, nor consumer credit to buy a refrigerator or a cooking stove! In such a desperate situation, the appropriate question is: What is the appropriate role of the government and the private sector in building a credible central bank and a modern financial system to address the real development challenges?

A vast literature shows that financial sector development can make an important contribution to economic growth and poverty reduction. This especially applies to the Democratic Republic of the Congo, whose financial sector is particularly underdeveloped, and without it economic development will certainly be constrained, even if other necessary conditions such as the rule of law, solid democratic institutions, infrastructure, lasting peace and human capital are met.

Central banks exist under difficult circumstances and are caught between the need to deliver price stability and being attentive to legitimate government demands. A reliable and stable currency is not only an advantage to the economy, but also, in particular, to the general public. Otmar Emminger, a former President of the Deutsche Bundesbank, expressed this aptly when he said that 'price stability is not everything, but without price stability everything is nothing'.

Some central banks are successful and others are not. This fact raises the question of the appropriate set up of a central bank in an emerging democracy with the goal of maximizing the chances of success. Is there an ideal model of central banking in a democracy? Can and should independence be traded off with accountability to achieve the goal of price stability and the stability of the financial sector, while addressing at the same time the pressures and demands of a democratic government?

What can be done to grow an inefficient central bank into a powerful institution that not only will be listened to, but also able to capitalize on its credibility to deliver results on its mandated goals? What can realistically be done for an emerging democracy to enjoy a strong and stable currency? If the existing financial system is not satisfactory, which institutions – both public and private – are necessary and how can they be created to grow in a sustainable manner to meet the country's development challenges?

A credible central bank can effectively lead the process of financial sector reform in a country so as to respond to these needs. This book lays out a vision for the reform of the central bank and the financial sector to make them useful tools for the development of any country, and of the Democratic Republic of the Congo in particular. Contrary to the conventional wisdom, I am advocating the view that, in an emerging democracy, the government has a responsibility to set the financial sector reform agenda instead of waiting for obscure instructions, diktats and conditionalities from afar, conditionalities which, in practice, have never been successful anywhere in the world.

For the sake of credibility, it is critical to clarify the relationship of central banks with governments, to explain the nature, degree of, and rationale for the independence afforded to many central banks – with a special focus on the role of the Central Bank of the Congo within the Congolese government – and to discuss the trade-off between independence and accountability in principle and in practice. I develop the process for an emerging country to build progressively and consciously a credible central bank that can achieve its mandated goal.

The primary goal of a central bank is to develop and maintain an efficient monetary system whose primary goal is price and financial stability, but it remains an open question as to what an ideal central bank should look like. Most high-income countries, and many low- and middle-income countries, have achieved success in maintaining low inflation and price stability, even though there are substantial differences in the organization, structure and functioning of their central banks. An institution as important as a central bank cannot take a particular form without substantial public understanding of the reasons for that form. The point to emphasize is that success on the inflation front is necessary if the central bank is to stabilize short-run fluctuations in real economic activity. Thus, it makes sense to assign a central bank an objective of contributing to real economic stability as long as it does not jeopardize the inflation objective.

The central bank's control of money and credit conditions in the economy is the core of what is referred to as monetary policy. This process of injecting or withdrawing liquidity in the financial markets accelerates or retards output growth and alters inflation pressures in the economy.

Monetary policy is a dynamic process, set with due consideration for the current conditions in the national economy. To achieve its goals, the central bank must ascertain where the economy is, where it is headed, and whether that direction is appropriate. If not, the central bank must take action to attempt to move the economy in a direction that is more consistent with its long-run objectives. This process requires constant vigilance and continual interaction with the markets to maintain financial conditions that are appropriate for maximum sustainable growth and price stability.

To apply these principles to a specific emerging democracy, I look at the case of the Democratic Republic of the Congo. The Central Bank of the Congo has three principal instruments at its disposal – the *taux directeur* or discount rate, direct open market operations, and reserve requirements – that can be used in support of these objectives.

The Central Bank of the Congo receives by design an appropriation from Parliament. But because it is viewed as a bankers' bank, it has to move progressively, once it is adequately capitalized, to fund itself from the return on its assets and from fees for its services to banks. It is the Central Bank's self-funding mechanism that has now planted the seeds of change that ultimately can lead to the emergence of the Monetary Policy Committee (MPC) or a National Open Market Committee (NOMC) as the primary monetary policy-making body.

If the Congolese financial system is to develop smoothly, and the economy is to join the modern industrialized world, the restructured Central Bank of the Congo will have to be much more than a storage facility for currency and priceless objects. Together with the elected government under the third Republic, the Central Bank of the Congo will have to manage a transition from the old dictatorial-style central bank, crafting the necessary market-based institutions, and setting in place a framework capable of delivering stable long-term growth in a sustainable manner.

To achieve financial stability, the Central Bank of the Congo needs to encourage the development of a sound banking system based on arm's-length relationships and market incentives. This means chartering banks to prevent unsavoury characters from running them, and setting up a system of supervision that penalizes bad business decisions and exercises strict quality control at entry in the financial sector. Then there are the day-to-day services that the Central Bank will have to provide. These include both the more mundane job of exchanging old, worn currency for new, crisp notes, and the technologically complex task of providing a payments network that allows funds to move among banks and across the country. The creation of an electronic payments system is essential to the process of intermediation. It will persuade individuals to deposit funds into banks and, in turn, encourage banks to make loans. To ensure that the payments system develops, the government and the Central Bank of the Congo should subsidize the interbank payments system, at least initially, making it cheaper and easier for commercial banks to serve their retail customers. As the financial system expands, the costs of running the payment system will have to be shared by the market participants.

Success in policy-making is as much an issue of institutional environment as of the people who are put in charge. Over the past several decades, economists have come to a consensus about the best way to design a central bank so that the people running it can be successful. A central bank must be independent of political pressures, accountable to the public, transparent in its policy actions, and a clear communicator with financial markets and the public. There is also agreement that it is prudent to have policy decisions made by committee rather than by a single individual or the governor alone.

Of these requirements, independence is by far the most important. In fact, virtually every high inflation episode in the world, including the Congolese hyperinflation that averaged 139 per cent per year for the period 1997–2007, is a direct consequence of the political subjugation of the central bank. Without alternative sources of revenue, governments turn to the central bank for financing, forcing them to print more and more money. The result, not surprisingly, is high rates of inflation. So the first step in achieving economic stability is to take the printing presses away from the politicians.

Accountability, transparency and communications become crucial once the central bank has been made independent. While the manner in which these goals are pursued depends critically on local culture and therefore differs across countries, a few things are universal. First, the public announcement of targets for the central bank is the only way to generate credibility. Second, the central bank has to publish key statistics regularly. Many credible central banks publish their balance sheets weekly, and the Central Bank of the Congo would be well advised to do the same thing in the future on a consistent basis. But in the end, exactly what they say and how they say it should depend on what works best with the Congolese people.

Without fiscal discipline, monetary policy is helpless. Looking at the Democratic Republic of the Congo today, I see immediately that this creates a serious risk. Rebuilding the country's physical infrastructure and transforming its economy into a market-based system is going to be very expensive. During the reconstruction phase, the Central Bank is going to be pressured to print money to finance the widening fiscal deficits. It is absolutely essential to find a way to avoid this and to prevent it from happening. My inclination is that the government should take charge of fiscal policy during the reconstruction, giving the Central Bank of the Congo some breathing space to confront the inflation problems it will inevitably face. The hope is that the restructured Central Bank of the Congo will be able to control inflation in the short term, thereby building the credibility that will be essential to a successful long-term inflation-targeting regime.

The task of maintaining price and monetary stability, the most common objective of central banks, is an immense one. We need to jettison the belief that all the functions that a central bank in an emerging democracy currently performs in meeting this objective are necessarily those it should continue to perform going forward. Achieving efficiency of operations dictates that a credible central bank performs only those underlying functions necessary to achieve this objective. These functions are to be carefully selected after a detailed review of the central bank operations in an effort to improve their efficiency.

If the Congolese people do what the Germans or the Americans did in setting up the Bundesbank (see Appendix 2) or the Federal Reserve System, or what the Europeans did in setting up the European Central Bank, then there is no alternative to transforming the Central Bank of the Congo into a powerful and credible central bank. Were that to happen, the Congolese currency could become as good as the euro or the dollar. This transformation cannot be accidental, however. It must be a part of the country's strategic vision for the financial sector, and it must fit into the country's long-term development agenda, something that the Congolese citizens alone can agree upon.

The development of the Congo requires a new focus on ways to encourage and remove barriers to wider formal financial sector provision of services. It also means that we should completely rethink the structure and functioning of the overall financial system in the Democratic Republic of the Congo to meet the needs, not of the colonial era, but of a truly independent country and its population. This also implies that, when designing regulatory reform (for example to promote stability or security), greater attention needs to be paid to the incentives and regulatory space affecting private sector financial institutions. Better data on access to financial services are also required in order to understand the development needs of the country, to identify the barriers to the wider formal sector, identify the kind of institutions that are needed and that can make the difference, and motivate the government and the private sector to take action to support the development of the financial sector and facilitate wider access by contributing to the implementation of well understood action plans. The strategic vision for the financial sector of the Democratic Republic of the Congo ought to propose a new structure for the Congolese financial and banking system to address in a lasting and sustainable manner the development challenges of the country and its people.

Developing the financial sector of the Democratic Republic of the Congo must be planned and the plan must be clearly understood and carefully implemented over time. One has first to visualize the type of system that the country needs for its development before that system can be implemented. Because the current system is known to be insufficient, inadequate and out of date, the plan should be implemented over a ten-year period. The plan should result in a strong currency and a diversified and well-functioning financial system. My 'vision for a strong currency' provides additional elements of the reform agenda designed to promote the Congolese franc to the position of a credible currency. The agenda is complemented by reforms designed to stabilize the exchange rate, reduce inflation, restructure the overall denominations of the national currency and introduce coins, as well as to promote the efficiency of the payments system.

All these reforms are to be driven by medium and long-term objectives to ensure economic prosperity for the Democratic Republic of the Congo, and for the country to become one of Africa's financial centres within the next twenty-five years. Only a sustained stable macroeconomic environment and a sound and vibrant financial system can propel the economy to achieve the Congo's desire to become one of the 50 largest economies in the world within the next thirty years. The strategic plan for the financial sector in the Congo will have three main components: currency reform or an agenda for the Congolese franc, central bank reform and the reconfiguration of the financial system. The agenda for the Congolese franc should therefore be launched as one of the three phases of the strategic plan for the financial sector in the quest by the Democratic Republic of the Congo to become an international financial centre and Africa's important financial hub.

The Congo should be working towards greater transparency in the formulation and implementation of its monetary policy and financial sector policies. The performance of the current Board of Directors of the Central Bank in the area of monetary policy remains questionable in light of the recent high rates of inflation. A new Monetary Policy Committee (MPC) needs to be constituted in accordance with the new Central Bank Act, and the minutes of the MPC should be made public.

It therefore goes without saying that if the Congolese currency is properly aligned and can become a 'reference currency', the goal of an African Monetary Union becomes all the more credible and sustainable. The Congo has met some of the convergence criteria and hopes to continue working towards these broad goals on a sustained basis. In the meantime, it must continue to make progress by strengthening its currency and keeping inflation very low.

The Congolese financial system is not to be restructured, but must be redesigned to comprise bank and non-bank financial institutions which would be regulated by the Ministry of Finance, the Central Bank of the Congo, the Congo Deposit Insurance Corporation, the Congo Securities and Exchange Commission, the National Insurance Commission, the National Mortgage Bank of the Congo, and the National Board for Community Banks. Of all these proposed regulatory agencies, the Central Bank of the Congo must have broad and wide-ranging supervisory powers over all the segments of the financial systems that can pose a threat or risk to the stability of the system as a whole. The Central Bank must introduce legislation that would allow the operation of more banks from other countries on a reciprocal basis.

There is a need to create a money market in the Congo. This is a market for short-term debt instruments. The major function of the money market would be to facilitate the raising of short-term funds from the surplus sectors to the deficit sectors of the economy. Money market institutions would constitute the hub of the financial system. These institutions would include discount houses, commercial and merchant banks, microfinance institutions and special purpose banks, such as community banks. Because these institutions do not exist at present, they will have to be created with a strong hand from the government in its catalytic role.

Developing the Congolese capital market is a matter of priority and urgency. The Congolese capital market would be a channel for mobilizing long-term funds. The main institutions in the market could include the Securities and Exchange Commission, which would be at the apex and serve as the regulatory authority of the market, the Kinshasa Stock

Exchange to be created as a matter of urgency, the issuing houses and the stockbroking firms. The capital market could be classified into primary and secondary segments.

The Democratic Republic of the Congo should aim to launch the Kinshasa Stock Exchange within the next three years. To encourage small as well as large-scale enterprises to gain access to public listing, the KSE could operate the main exchange for relatively large enterprises, and for small and medium-sized enterprises. Listing requirements for small and medium enterprises would be made less stringent to facilitate their participation in the market. Clear signs could notify the public as to what requirements have been adapted to facilitate the listing of small and medium-sized enterprises.

Specialized banks or development finance institutions should be established to contribute to the development of specific sectors of the economy. They would consist of the International Bank for the Reconstruction and Development of the Democratic Republic of the Congo, the Congo Industrial Development Bank, the Congo Bank for Commerce and Industry, the Congo Agricultural and Cooperative Bank, and the Urban Development Bank. Like other financial institutions, all development banks would be under the supervision of the Central Bank of the Congo.

There are or would be other institutions and funds within the financial system that play important intermediating roles. The institutions would include: insurance companies, finance companies, exchange bureaux, primary mortgage institutions, industrial promotion funds, Congolese social insurance funds, and national security funds.

Many of these institutions are non-existent today. If the institution does not exist and if the private sector has not created it or is not ready for it, it ought to be created by the government with a view to selling it later to private shareholders once conditions permit. While many so-called conservative economists might take offence at my advocating a greater role for the government in the financial sector than they might wish to hear, I question the wisdom of the usual hands-off approach advocated by the traditional conditionalities-driven interventions which, in practice, have never been successful anywhere in the world.

Preface

Throughout much of my professional career, I have worked on economic and financial sector issues that affect central banks and financial systems directly or indirectly. My earliest involvement in this area dealt with the restructuring of financial systems in several countries and the conditions that lead to hyperinflation and their end point, an extreme situation of total subjugation of a central bank to government demands. By 1997, when the Democratic Republic of the Congo changed its political leadership and began preparing a comprehensive monetary reform, I became more interested in the relationship between central banks and governments as well as the monetary policy choices made by these same authorities. I saw the Congo introducing the Congolese franc at the rate of one dollar to 1.3 francs in June 1998. By June 2007, the exchange rate had become 565 francs to the dollar. A currency which was supposed to be strong had become almost worthless within a ten-year period.

Parallel literatures, with important contributions by economists specializing in emerging countries, had emerged wherein a central bank was either an optimizing agent that could fine-tune the economy, or behaved as a bureaucratic institution determined to maintain its special role via obfuscation and secrecy. At the same time, political economists and political scientists have shown that central banks were constantly pressured by the political authorities to change their policies to facilitate a sizeable victory during the democratic elections or to support partisan economic programmes.

Little did I know in 1993 that a topic that remained largely dormant in economists' minds (but not in the minds of political scientists) would get its second wind so to speak. The catalyst was the publication of John Taylor's article on the Federal Reserve System and its interest rate setting behaviour. This led to an explosion of research into the 'new' economics of central bank reaction functions. As part of this renewed interest in central banking studies, I undertook in 1997 a research programme at the Université de Paris IX–Dauphine, to investigate the relationship between central bank independence, accountability and their impact on monetary policy. To be practical, I made my research applicable to my home country, the Democratic Republic of the Congo. The dissertation was published extensively in 2001 in international and Congolese magazines and newspapers and contributed in various ways to the debate on the need for greater autonomy of the Central Bank. By January 2002, the transitional Parliament of the Democratic Republic of the Congo passed the law granting independence to the Central Bank of the Congo. This was the first time that the country had passed such a law.

Since that time, I have observed closely how central banks react to both the economic and political pressures they face. Several central banks live under difficult conditions and are caught between the need to deliver price stability and at the same time to be attentive to legitimate government demands. Some central banks are successful and others are not. This book addresses the issues of the appropriate set up of a central bank in an emerging democracy with a view to maximizing its chances of success. Is there an ideal model of central banking in a democracy? Can and should independence be traded off with accountability to achieve the goal of price stability and the stability of the financial sector, while addressing at the same time the pressures and demands of a democratic government? What can be done to transform a dysfunctional central bank into an effective institution that not only can be listened to, but can capitalize on its credibility to deliver results on its mandated goals?

A credible central bank can effectively lead the process of financial sector reform in a country. A large body of evidence now exists which shows that financial sector development can make an important contribution to economic growth and poverty reduction. This is especially true in the Democratic Republic of the Congo, whose financial sector is particularly underdeveloped, and without it economic development will be difficult. Insufficient financial development may leave the Democratic Republic of the Congo in a 'poverty trap'. Because of increasing returns to scale in the financial sector, a vicious circle might be created, where low levels of financial intermediation result in only a few financial market participants. Lack of competition results in high costs, leading to low real deposit rates and hence low savings, which in turn limit the amount of financial intermediation. Financial sector underdevelopment can therefore be a serious obstacle to growth in the Democratic Republic of the Congo, even when the country has established other conditions necessary for sustained economic development.

This book will attempt to lay out a vision for the reform of the Central Bank and the financial sector to make them useful tools for the development of any country, and of the Democratic Republic of the Congo in particular. In this book, I suggest that the government should take responsibility and lead the efforts to reform the financial sector instead of waiting for obscure instructions, diktats and conditionalities from afar, conditionalities which, in practice, have never been successful anywhere in the world.

Dr Noël K. Tshiani
Washington, D.C., April 2008

About the Author

Noël K. Tshiani is a World Bank Country Manager. He has been a World Bank Professional staff for the last sixteen years. During a year of sabbatical in 2007, he served as president of Companie Financière d'Investissement et du Crédit, LLC. Prior to this position, he worked for the World Bank as a senior task team leader, and served as World Bank Resident Representative in Chad from 2004 to 2006. He had previously been an international lending officer with Citibank and JPM Chase for eight years. Dr Tshiani completed the New Managers Leadership Program at the Graduate Business School at Harvard University in Boston–Massachusetts, and holds a Doctorate in Economics with specialization in Banking and Finance from Université de Paris IX-Dauphine in France, a Master's Degree in Business Administration (MBA) with concentration in Banking and Financial Markets from Adephi University in New York, and a Master's Degree in Economics from Université de Liège in Belgium. He is the author of the 2008 book *Vision pour une Monnaie Forte: Plaidoyer pour une nouvelle politique monétaire au Congo.*

List of Abbreviations

ADB	African Development Bank
BCC	Banque Centrale du Congo
BCEAO	Banque centrale des Etats de l'Afrique de l'Ouest (Central Bank of West African States)
BEAC	Banque des Etats de l'Afrique Centrale (Bank of Central African States)
CACB	Congo Agricultural and Cooperative Bank
CBCI	Congo Bank for Commerce and Industry
CD	Certificate of Deposit
CDIC	Congo Deposit Insurance Corporation
CEAC	Communauté des Etats d'Afrique Centrale
CFA	Cooperation Financière en Afrique
CIDB	Congo Industrial Development Bank
CP	Commercial Paper
CPI	Consumer Price Index
CSEC	Congo Securities and Exchange Commission
CSITF	Congo Social Insurance Trust Fund
DFI	Development Finance Institution
DIF	Deposit Insurance Fund
DIS	Deposit Insurance Scheme
DRC	Democratic Republic of the Congo
ECB	European Central Bank
ECOFIN	Economic and Financial Council
EIB	European Investment Bank
EMU	European Monetary Union
ERM	Exchange Rate Mechanism
ESCB	European System of Central Banks
EU	European Union
FOMC	Federal Open Market Committee
FSCC	Financial Services Coordinating Committee
GDP	Gross Domestic Product
IBRDC	International Bank for the Reconstruction and Development of the Congo
IFAD	International Fund for Agricultural Development
INSS	National Social Security Institute
IPF	Industrial Promotion Fund

KSE	Kinshasa Stock Exchange
MBO	Management by objective
MF	Ministry of Finance
MPC	Monetary Policy Committee
NIC	National Insurance Commission
NMBC	National Mortgage Bank of the Congo
NOMC	National Open Market Committee
OMO	Open Market Operation
PMI	Primary Mortgage Institution
RPI	Retail Price Index
SME	Small and medium-sized enterprises
SONAS	Société Nationale d'Assurance
UDB	Urban Development Bank
UEMOA	Union Economique et Monétaire Ouest Africaine (West African Economic and Monetary Union)

Introduction

Financial sector development can make an important contribution to economic growth and poverty reduction in the Democratic Republic of the Congo. However, at present the financial sector there is particularly underdeveloped, and therefore its economic development is constrained. It is generally believed today that, throughout the world, 'independence' is a prerequisite for achieving the goals that traditionally have been assigned to central banks – specifically for achieving price stability. But the meaning of central bank independence is often misunderstood, which leads to reluctance by the legislators and political elite in developing countries to embrace it convincingly. 'Central bank independence' does not mean literally independence from government, because central banks in the Democratic Republic of the Congo and abroad are almost always part of the government. The relationship of central banks to the rest of government is, in practice, much more complex than the term 'independence' might suggest.

The rationale for granting independence to central banks is to insulate the conduct of monetary policy from political interference, especially interference motivated by the pressures of elections to deliver short-term gains irrespective of longer-term costs. As *The Economist* noted nearly twenty years ago, 'The only good central bank is one that can say **NO** to politicians' (10 February 1990). The intent of this insulation, however, is not to free the central bank to pursue whatever policy it prefers – indeed every country specifies the goals of monetary policy to some degree – but to provide a credible commitment of the government, through its central bank, to achieving those goals, especially price stability.

Even a limited degree of independence, taken literally, could be viewed as inconsistent with democratic ideals and, in addition, might leave the central bank without appropriate incentives to carry out its responsibilities. Therefore, independence has to be balanced or traded off with accountability – accountability of the central bank to the public and, specifically, to its elected representatives such as senators or members of the National Assembly.

It is important to appreciate, however, that steps to encourage accountability also offer opportunities for political pressure. The history of the Central Bank of the Congo's relationship to the rest of government is one marked by efforts by the rest of government both to reduce central bank independence by controlling it and to exert political pressure on monetary policy.

The purpose of this book is to clarify the relationship of central banks within government, to explain the nature, degree of, and rationale for the independence afforded to many central banks – with a special focus on the role of the Central Bank of the Congo within the Congolese government – and to discuss the trade-off between independence and accountability in principle and in practice. The book demonstrates the process by which an emerging country can build progressively and consciously a credible central bank to achieve the goal of price stability on one side, and financial stability more broadly on the other.

1
Is There an Ideal Set Up for a Central Bank?

The primary goal of a central bank is to develop and maintain an efficient monetary system whose primary goal is price stability, but it remains an open question as to what an ideal central bank should look like. The answer to this question is important, but it would be a bad mistake to believe that there is only one best way to organize a central bank in an emerging democracy. Most high-income countries, and many low- and middle-income countries, have achieved success in maintaining low inflation and price stability, even though there are substantial differences in the organization, structure and functioning of their central banks. We need to think out of the box about the design of the central bank and recognize that there are different ways to achieve the same end. Success in achieving low and stable inflation – price stability – is relatively recent in a number of countries. We may well discover that some institutional arrangements are more robust over time than others, as we observe how various arrangements stand up to stresses not yet observed.

An institution as important as a central bank cannot take a particular form without substantial public understanding of the reasons for that form. A century ago, most people believed that the only sound basis for a monetary system was for paper money to be convertible into gold. Yet, adherence to the gold standard during the early 1930s led to a large deflation that contributed to the Great Depression. Looking back today, we see that the countries that stayed with the gold standard the longest had the worst depressions. Throughout the Depression in major industrial countries, a number of economists argued that central banks should not be constrained by a rigid link to gold, but the economists could not sway public opinion which resisted any fundamental changes from the established practices.

For some years after World War Two, most observers believed that fixed exchange rates were essential to monetary stability. And, therefore, governments around the world were able to set up an international monetary system in which a central bank's primary job was to monitor and maintain a fixed exchange rate vis-à-vis the American dollar. But, for an individual country, maintaining a fixed exchange rate vis-à-vis the American dollar was tantamount to accepting the inflation consequences of American monetary policy, which led many countries to realize that they were paying a very high price for their adherence to the system by supporting the heavy cost of American economic mismanagement. This system failed because the United States followed a monetary policy that yielded an inflation rate considered unacceptably high by some important countries.

In both cases, bankers, economists and policy-makers lobbied for institutional changes long before they became politically feasible. We see today in many countries, and particularly in emerging democracies, potential reforms (such as setting a target for inflation) that we believe would improve their central banks' economic performance. But such changes are still difficult to make because popular opinion and understanding of economic ideas impose limits on policy-makers' ability to transform the economy and the central bank by changing laws. In a country such as the Democratic Republic of the Congo (DRC) that has recently gone through its first multi-party democratic elections in 50 years, the challenge of setting up an ideal central bank with a clear mandate and freedom to achieve that mandate is made even more difficult. It requires mobilizing public opinion, including educating the political elite and intellectuals to the need to make changes in order to insulate the central bank from political pressure and domination. The changes include, among others, not only the laws affecting the functioning of a central bank, but also encouraging the public's aversion to inflation and educating the population as to the real purpose of a central bank, how to evaluate its performance and what constitute in practice the criteria for a successful monetary policy.

Historical perspective

The logical place to begin an analysis of how to design an optimal central bank law is with a simple statement of economic principles that should guide the thinking:

- Inflation – anticipated and especially unanticipated – above some threshold rate is costly. Deflation is also costly. The costs of departures are not symmetric; deflation of 4 per cent per year is likely to be much more costly than inflation of 4 per cent per year.

- There is no long-run trade-off between inflation and unemployment, and the short-run trade-off may be too unreliable to be useful for policy-makers.
- Market expectations about future monetary policy (and future economic policies generally) are extremely important in determining how well monetary policy will work.
- Freedom of action is important for a central bank's decisions to be effective.

Central bank activities

Because inflation and deflation are costly, a central bank ought to have an explicit inflation target. In an emerging democracy such as the Democratic Republic of the Congo, some economists believe that the appropriate target is zero inflation, properly measured – that is, after accounting for measurement errors in price indexes. We believe that a small, positive rate of inflation is appropriate. The difference between 0 and, say, 4 per cent inflation per year is a minor matter relative to other issues. In particular, reasonable stability in the rate of inflation and especially in the expected rate of inflation over the medium term is more important than whether the target is 0 or 4 per cent per year. Whether the target is expressed as a point or a range is an interesting issue, but it is not fundamental.

The weight of public opinion must be behind the idea of an inflation target, whether it is legislated or not. If the public does not support the target, the target will not be effective, even if it is legislated. The Democratic Republic of the Congo does not have a legislated target, but since 1997 following the latest monetary reform, the Central Bank of the Congo (Banque Centrale du Congo – BCC) has not been successful in achieving and maintaining a low average rate of inflation despite some unrealistically conceived targets imposed by international organizations through stabilization programmes. What is needed in a country such as the Democratic Republic of the Congo is not so much a legislated inflation target but a target framework that the public regards as having constitutional force.

A law or a practice has constitutional force if it cannot be changed without resorting to lengthy discussion and, in the case of a law, by a super majority or its equivalent. For example, in the United States, the gold standard once had constitutional force even though it was never written into the Constitution explicitly.

In many countries, debate over a legislated inflation target has been extremely valuable in helping to create a consensus of constitutional force. In this debate, central bankers and others must constantly explain the reasons for a legislated target to ensure that it is not simply absorbed into the immense mass of legislation that is widely ignored and largely forgotten.

Not only must central bankers continually explain such a need, they must be consistent in this explanation – and in all of their policy explanations. Such consistent policies build credibility and market confidence over time. If credibility is lost, regaining it takes time and a willingness to endure short-run pain where the short run may be measured in years. Maintaining credibility over time requires institutional strength that transcends current central bank leadership. Absent crisis conditions, policy should evolve relatively slowly over time, with each change studied carefully and then explained fully. Otherwise, the predictability upon which credibility depends may be incomplete. The purpose of sustained low inflation is to minimize price level shocks that upset business planning and that redistribute income and wealth arbitrarily. For the same reason, the central bank should strive to avoid surprises in its own policy procedures.

One of the most difficult and hotly debated issues is whether monetary policy should be confined to an inflation objective or should also have an employment or growth objective. It does not make economic sense for the central bank to have objectives stated in terms of the level of employment or the rate of growth of real GDP. It is within the power of the central bank to achieve a long-run inflation objective, but not to achieve an objective for the level of employment or the real GDP growth rate. In the long run, the level of employment and economic growth are determined by non-monetary factors such as capital accumulation, advances in science and technology, well-defined property rights and other regulations that allow markets to work well. No organization should be assigned an objective that it cannot achieve or, at best, can achieve only temporarily.

The Central Bank of the Congo does have the power, however, to contribute to employment stability. Historically, the largest spells of high unemployment have followed periods in which the Central Bank of the Congo lost control of inflation and had to raise interest rates very high to regain control. Preventing these bouts of high inflation is the best way to avoid having bouts of high unemployment. Provided that the central bank's short-run policy decisions do not shake confidence in the long-run policy, it can direct short-run policy to help cushion employment fluctuations. It is reasonable to interpret a number of episodes in the Democratic Republic of the Congo since 1997 in this way; most recently, it appears that the BCC's reduction of its reserve requirement in 2006 did not much help the extent of the economic slowdown and went widely unnoticed. And recent changes in the level of *taux directeur* by the BCC occurred without much effect on the economy. Of course, we cannot judge the success of a policy by one single incomplete episode.

The point to emphasize is that success on the inflation front is necessary if the central bank is to stabilize short-run fluctuations in real economic activity. Thus, it makes sense to assign a central bank an objective of contributing to real economic stability as long as it does not jeopardize the inflation objective. The Central Bank of the Congo operates under a vague legislated instruction – vague in the sense that no numerical targets are specified – to contribute to achieving high employment and price stability. If the statutory language is interpreted as suggested above, then such objectives make perfectly good sense.

A legislated employment stabilization objective complicates the relationship between the elected government officials and the central bank because the central bank must maintain a long horizon. That horizon is typically considerably longer than the horizon of elected officials, who quite naturally and understandably have an intense focus on the next election. Because of the way the economy works, a central bank must be willing to back away from efforts to stabilize income and employment when such efforts threaten the inflation objective. Failing to maintain the primacy of the inflation objective only puts economic stability at risk over the longer run. The Democratic Republic of the Congo and many other countries had ample experience with this scenario in the 1990s; excesses in short-run recession fighting created higher inflation over the longer run and deeper recessions later on.

Freedom and authority to do what is right

There is widespread agreement that central bank independence leads to better monetary policy. The logic of independence can be seen by looking at the different horizons of elected officials and of central banks. Democratic leaders compete for office promising change and improvement rather than continuity and stability, whereas an incoming head of a central bank will almost certainly want to continue the policies of a successful predecessor and will emphasize his or her commitment to do so. Political independence and non-partisan monetary policy provide the promise of policy stability over time, which in turn stabilizes expectations in asset markets. Such stability and continuity are essential to a successful monetary policy.

Central bank independence requires that the head of the bank have a substantial term of office and that individual policy decisions are not subject to revision by the government. However, such structural features of the central bank's institutional design are only the starting point for central bank independence. If the government publicly attacks the central bank's policies, then independence will certainly be incomplete. This subject is a very difficult one for an emerging democratic society: How can an important area of public policy be off-limits for comment and criticism by elected officials? Yet, such criticism clearly unsettles markets and damages the effectiveness of monetary policy.

One way around this problem is for the government to exercise great forbearance and confine its criticism to internal discussions with the central bank. That has yet to become the tradition in the Democratic Republic of the Congo, as the practice has not been established long enough that it can be regarded as institutionalized. Consideration of this issue makes clear that optimal central bank design in an emerging democracy goes far beyond legal issues per se; it is ludicrous to consider the possibility of passing a law saying that the government is not allowed to comment on central bank policy! Clearly, though, if the government does not retain confidence in the central bank, the country is in substantial trouble. In this situation, the government must be prepared to replace promptly a failing central bank leadership when terms of office expire.

Although central banks have governmental functions, the most successful banks are those with the fewest political overtones. The organization of the Federal Reserve System fits this perspective very nicely. Members of its Board of Governors are appointed by the president of the United States and confirmed by the Senate. However, presidents of the Reserve banks are appointed by the directors of the Reserve banks, subject to approval by the Fed's Board of Governors. Directors of Reserve banks have powers and responsibilities that are closer to those of a private company than those of a government agency. At each Reserve bank, six of the nine directors are elected by the commercial banks that are members of the Reserve bank; the other three directors are appointed by the Board of Governors on the recommendation of the Reserve bank. The directors are explicitly non-political; they are drawn from the local community and are not permitted to hold partisan political office or to participate in political activity, such as heading campaign committees or leading political fund-raising efforts. The directors, in turn, select the bank president and first vice-president, subject to approval by the Board of Governors.

This institutional arrangement clearly involves ultimate control of the Federal Reserve System through the political process centred on the Board of Governors. Yet, a considerable part of the System's leadership obtains office through what is essentially a private-sector process. What this private-sector process does is to reinforce the non-political nature of the central bank. The process also involves the central bank directors in an important way. The central bank pays the bank directors very little; what they get out of their term as director is the opportunity for public service that includes an intense education in monetary policy. Over their years of service, and for years thereafter, the directors spread knowledge of monetary policy processes and challenges throughout their communities. Having community leaders from many different professions serving as directors builds support for sound monetary policy. Consider, for example, the breadth of experience on the board of the Central Bank of the Congo if directors are drawn from every sector of the economy and every geographic region of the country on the basis of their expertise and competence.

Equally important to the Central Bank of the Congo is the flow of information from its branch managers to the bank's governor and other board members, who in turn use this information to make decisions on monetary policy. Valuable information also comes from numerous advisory committees that meet from time to time at the Board of Directors' gatherings, and from contacts between the central bank officials and their audiences as the officials travel to speak at various events and meet with business and community leaders. The Central Bank of the Congo must develop grassroots contacts throughout the country and continuously over time. Developing a central organization along these ideas in the Congo will contribute greatly to the prospects for continued sound monetary policy in the years ahead.

Openness

In recent years, central banks have become more open in many different ways. In the past, central bankers often discussed monetary policy in obscure ways and seemed to relish the mystique of central banking. Given central bank independence, openness is essential to political accountability. Whether by law or by confirmed practice, good central bank design calls for central banks to make timely reports about policy actions, including the reasons for these changes.

Importantly, prompt disclosure of policy decisions and their rationale is necessary for markets to function efficiently. Monetary policy works through financial markets; if markets expect one policy direction when the central bank intends another, both the markets and the central bank are likely to be surprised at some point and disappointed by the results.

Conclusion

There is no uniquely optimal way to write a central bank law and to institutionalize central bank practices. Different countries have different histories and different preferences. Among those successful in promoting price stability and economic growth, there are three common elements.

First, the government should assign clear and realistic objectives to the central bank. A legislated inflation target is a good idea, but more important than legislation is an understanding in the society that low and stable inflation is the central bank's responsibility and that the bank should be judged on how well it achieves that objective. A government may assign to the central bank a policy goal of contributing to stability in income and employment, provided there is a clear understanding that there can be no central bank target for the level of employment or the rate of growth in gross domestic product (GDP).

Second, the central bank should operate independently within the government; the head of the bank should have a reasonably long term of office and should not be subject to removal by the elected head of government, except for valid cause through an impeachment process. The head of government should not be able to overturn individual monetary policy decisions and, ideally, should confine comment on those decisions to confidential communications with the central bank.

Third, the central bank should be transparent in the way it makes decisions and implements policy. Political accountability requires transparency, as does the efficient operation of the markets through which monetary policy affects the economy.

These three principles broadly characterize all major central banks today and have to be incorporated in the design of an ideal central bank in an emerging democracy. We should not, however, take that fact as reason to assume that the issue is settled. We are bound to face stresses in the future when many will question these principles which are tantamount to a new style in central banking. Stating them now, defending them and explaining them represent our best hope for improving public understanding and maintaining the progress of recent years that is so evident to all central banks. But this is not so evident to policy-makers in a number of countries. This book is part of the effort to raise awareness of these fundamental principles for the establishment of an ideal central bank in emerging democracies, including the Democratic Republic of the Congo following the recent first multi-party elections since independence.

2
Central Bank Independence and Accountability: a Trade-off

The case for a credible and independent central bank is becoming increasingly accepted. This new orthodoxy is based on three foundations: the success of the Bundesbank and the German economy over the past 50 years and its successor, the European Central Bank; the theoretical academic literature on the inflationary bias of discretionary policy-making; and the empirical academic literature on central bank independence. The purpose of this chapter is to examine whether this accepted concept of independence can be traded off and balanced with a reasonable degree of accountability for a central bank in an emerging democracy such as the Democratic Republic of the Congo.

In this context, we will show that society will be better off if the central bank pre-commits to an inflation rate, provided the fiscal authority is reasonably well behaved. We tie these conclusions to the literature on optimal incentive contracts for central banks. Finally we draw a distinction between goal independence and instrument independence for the central bank. Given that a trade-off exists between output and inflation variability, the trade-off should not be left to the central bank, i.e. it should not have goal independence. Rather, the goals for the central bank should be clearly specified, so that the central bank can then be accountable for achieving these goals. However, it should be free in its choice of means to achieve these goals.

Central bank independence

The dictionary defines independence as being free from the influence, guidance or control of another or others. As applied to central banks, that translates into being free from the influence, guidance or control of the rest of government, meaning both the executive and legislative branches in the Democratic Republic of the Congo.

Central bank independence refers to three areas in which the influence of the government must be either excluded or drastically curtailed: independence in personnel matters, financial independence and independence with respect to policy.

Personnel independence refers to the influence the government of the Democratic Republic of the Congo has in personnel appointment procedures. It is not feasible to exclude government influence completely in appointments to a public institution as important as the Central Bank of the Congo. However, the level of this influence may be curtailed by criteria such as government representation on the BCC's governing board, and government guidelines for appointments procedures, terms of office, and dismissal of the governing board.

Financial independence refers to the ability given to the Central Bank of the Congo to finance its own expenditures directly. Direct access by the government to central bank credits implies that monetary policy is subordinated to fiscal policy. Indirect access may result because the BCC is cashier to the government and because it handles the management of government debt.

Policy independence refers to the room for manoeuvre given to the Central Bank of the Congo in the formulation and execution of monetary policy. Here it may be helpful to distinguish *independence with respect to goals* and *independence with respect to instruments*. Two related issues are important for independence with respect to goals: the scope that the Central Bank of the Congo has to exercise its own discretion and the presence or absence of monetary stability as the central bank's primary goal. If the central bank has been assigned various goals such as low inflation and low unemployment, it is believed that it has been accorded the greatest degree of discretion. In that case, the central bank is independent with respect to goals, because it is free to set the final goals of monetary policy. It may, for example, decide that price stability is less important than output stability and act accordingly in policy decision. However, if it is given either general or specific objectives with respect to price stability (this is currently the case of the Central Bank of the Congo whose goal of monetary policy is clearly spelled out in its statutes as price stability), the central bank's discretionary powers will be restricted. To defend its goals, a central bank must wield effective policy instruments. A bank is independent with respect to instruments if it is free to choose the means or instruments by which to achieve its goals. It is not independent if it requires government approval to use policy instruments. If the central bank is obliged to finance budget deficits, it also lacks instruments independence. In this regard, financial independence and instruments independence are related; instruments independence is broader, however, because it entails the power to set interest rates.

If a central bank is free to set the final objectives for monetary policy, it has goal independence. If a central bank is free to choose the settings for its instruments in order to pursue its ultimate objectives, it has instruments independence.

Most central banks have specific legislative mandates and therefore do not have goal independence. Thus the 'independence' of 'independent' central banks is instruments independence under which the central bank has authority to choose settings for its instruments in order to pursue the objectives mandated by the legislature, without seeking permission from, or being overturned by, either the executive or the legislature. However, countries vary considerably in the specificity of the mandated goals and hence in the degree of discretion of central banks in the conduct of monetary policy.

Is there a real need for central bank independence?

Central bank independence is designed to insulate the central bank from the short-term and often myopic political pressures associated with the electoral cycle. Elected officials have incentives to deliver benefits before the next election even if the associated costs might make them undesirable from a longer-term perspective. This phenomenon has been called the political business cycle in which pre-election stimulus leads to higher inflation followed by monetary restraint after the election.

On the other hand, it appears that elected officials in many countries apparently understand the incentives under which they operate and have structured charters for their central banks that, in effect, tie their own hands – that is, they limit political interference with monetary policy to enhance the prospects of achieving and maintaining price stability. Nevertheless, the urge to exert political pressure – to support the objectives of the administration as well as those of the Parliament, to take the Congolese case, and at other times to support the re-election of the president or of parliamentarian or senatorial incumbents – sometimes becomes irresistible. At such times, the tradition of independence at the Central Bank of the Congo, the leadership of its governor, the influence of long terms for members of the board, and the presence of representatives of all the country's financial districts on the National Open Market Committee (NOMC) or in the Monetary Policy Committee (MPC) could become especially important.

In addition, budget priorities and monetary policy objectives can be in conflict. The executive branch generally wants to keep the cost of servicing its debt low, and this preference might be at odds with the need for monetary policy to vary interest rates to maintain price stability. This tension has been present during the recent wars that the Congo experienced since 1997.

Finally, especially in countries where debt markets are not well developed, such as the case of the Democratic Republic of the Congo, central banks might be called upon to finance budget deficits by printing money, again interfering with the maintenance of price stability. The Central Bank of the Congo, for example, was asked to directly underwrite government debt by issuing new bank notes during the 1997 and 1998 wars. The central bank was in no position to say no to these demands because there was no statutory prohibition on directly purchasing government debt or on issuing uncovered additional central bank money. It is advisable that, in today's emerging democracy, such a prohibition[1] be clearly added by the legislators to the Central Bank of the Congo Act.

Some have worried that even an independent Central Bank of the Congo could succumb to the temptation to stimulate the economy today at the expense of higher inflation in the future. This is referred to as the problem of time inconsistency. That is, the Central Bank of the Congo has an incentive to commit itself to price stability and then to renege on this promise in order either to gain employment in the short run with relatively little initial sacrifice in the form of higher inflation (see Table 2.1), or simply to finance the budget deficits under government pressures. In the long run inflation would rise and the Central Bank of the Congo would either have to tolerate the higher rate of inflation or push output below potential for a while to restore price stability. Once the public understands this process, moreover, it would expect higher inflation, so that, in the longer run, the result could be higher inflation without any short-run gain in output.

Several solutions to the time inconsistency problem have been offered. First, the rest of the Congolese government could impose a rule on the Central Bank of the Congo, restricting its ability to play the game described above. The rule would ensure a credible commitment to price stability, thereby anchoring the public's expectations and removing the inflationary bias that otherwise might result. Second, the Congolese government could appoint conservative central bankers – central bankers

Table 2.1 DRC: inflation rates from 1990 to 2006 (%)

Year	*Inflation*
1990	264.9
1991	3,641.9
1992	2,989.6
1993	4,851.7
1994	9,796.9
1995	370.3
1996	693.0
1997	13.7
1998	134.8
1999	483.7
2000	522.2
2001	135.1
2002	15.8
2003	16.0
2004	14.0
2005	14.0
2006	22.0
2007	20.0

Source: Central Bank of the Congo.

with a greater commitment to price stability than the public – and thereby offset the inflationary bias that would otherwise arise. Third, central bankers could be forced to operate under performance or incentive contracts, whereby they could be penalized for failure to maintain price stability. If the governor of the Central Bank of the Congo operates under such a performance contract, he can be removed from office for failure to achieve his inflation target.

This author has never found the literature on time inconsistency particularly relevant to central banks. Surely central banks realize they are facing a repeated game, not a one-time game. They will therefore be reluctant to undermine their credibility over the longer run by pretending to pursue price stability while stimulating the economy for short-run gain. Long terms of office and other institutional ways of insulating central banks from short-term political pressures allow central bankers to take this longer view and make them less likely to follow time-inconsistent policies. Still, the problem highlighted in the time inconsistency literature may reinforce the case for both a price stability legislative mandate and instruments independence for the Central Bank of the Congo.

True and effective independence is also likely to reinforce the credibility of the Central Bank of the Congo's commitment to price stability. This enhanced credibility may then yield additional benefits. First, it could allow the BCC to reduce the cost of lowering inflation. It is generally agreed that to lower inflation monetary policy must reduce output for a while, relative to potential, by reducing aggregate demand. The resulting loss of output during the transition to lower inflation is a measure of the cost of reducing inflation. The more quickly inflation expectations fall, the more rapidly will inflation itself decline, and the lower will be the cost of reducing inflation.

A credible Central Bank of the Congo could also be more effective in conducting stabilization policy. If aggregate demand were to slow, a simulative monetary policy move would be less likely to undermine confidence in the BCC's pursuit of price stability when the central bank is independent (and has a price stability mandate). In addition, if inflation moved upward, inflation expectations would be less likely to follow immediately, making it easier for the Central Bank of the Congo to contain inflation.

Benefits of central bank independence

An extensive literature examines the relationship between the independence of the central bank and economic performance. The empirical studies generally find an inverse relationship between measures of central bank independence and both average inflation and variability of inflation, for both developed and developing economies. These are only correlations, however, and thus do not prove causation. The inverse relationship could also reflect the fact that countries with less aversion to inflation might be less likely to have independent central banks. This is the case for the Democratic Republic of the Congo where the large majority of people has taken in general a passive attitude towards inflation and the issues pertaining to the statutes of the Central Bank of the Congo. In addition, there is no consistent evidence of a relationship between central bank independence and real economic activity or consistent evidence that central bank independence lowers the cost of reducing inflation or increases the effectiveness of stabilization policy. On balance, the evidence for the benefits of central bank independence is strong enough to satisfy those who find theoretical arguments persuasive, although it is not strong enough to convince sceptics.

A history of central bank independence

A century ago there were only eighteen central banks, sixteen in Europe, plus Japan and Indonesia. Today there are 172 central banks and over recent years the number of central banks that claim some degree of independence from governments has steadily increased. More central banks have become independent in the 1990s than in any other decade since World War Two. The Central Bank of the Congo claimed its independence, at least on paper, since 2002.

The Bank of England

Changes in Britain, Japan, and continental Europe made 1998 a banner year in the history of central bank independence. The Bank of England, one of the oldest central banks in the world, was founded by an Act of Parliament in 1694. It was involved in commercial activity until the end of the nineteenth century, but it had gradually shifted during those 200 years towards an exclusive focus on central bank activity. The Bank of England had substantial independence for much of the eighteenth and nineteenth centuries, but by the twentieth century it had essentially become an agency of the British Treasury. Then, in June 1998, it was reborn as an independent central bank under the Labour government. It is credited for a sound monetary policy that explains the strength and credibility of the British pound as one of the world reserve currencies often surpassing or rivalling the American dollar or the European euro.

An independent Bank of England

In 1998, as well as modifying the inflation target, the new government gave the Bank of England independence to set interest rates. This was a major change in the policy framework. It meant that interest rates would no longer be set by politicians. The Bank would act independently of government, though the inflation target would be set by the Chancellor. The Bank would be accountable to Parliament and the wider public.

The objective given to the Bank of England was initially explained in a letter from the Chancellor. This objective was then formalized in the 1998 Bank of England Act. The Bank has 'to maintain price stability, and, subject to that, to support the economic policy of the Government including its objectives for growth and employment' (Bank of England Act 1998).

The Bank Act recognizes the role of price stability in achieving economic stability more generally, and in enabling sustainable growth in output and employment. It also recognizes that the inflation target will not be achieved all the time and that, confronted with unexpected developments in the economy, striving to meet the target in all circumstances might cause undesirable volatility of output.

The Chancellor restates the inflation target each year. From June 1997 to December 2003, the target was 2.5 per cent for retail price index (RPI) inflation. On 10 December 2003, the Chancellor changed the target to 2.0 per cent for consumer price index (CPI) inflation.

If the inflation target is missed by more than 1 percentage point on either side – in other words, if the annual rate of CPI inflation is more than 3.0 per cent or less than 1.0 per cent – the governor of the Bank, as chairman of the Monetary Policy Committee, must write an open letter to the Chancellor explaining the reasons why inflation has increased or fallen to such an extent and what the Bank proposes to do to ensure inflation comes back to the target. This does not mean that the Bank has a target of 1.0–3.0 per cent. The target is 2.0 per cent. But if inflation varies by more than 1 percentage point from the target, the Bank has to explain why.

So far this has not happened. But it is probable that at some point the annual rate of inflation will be more than 1 percentage point from the target. This is because, from time to time, the economy will face unexpected changes and be influenced by unforeseen events.

The Monetary Policy Committee

The Chancellor instructed the Bank to create a new committee to set interest rates – the Monetary Policy Committee composed of nine independent members: five from the Bank of England and four external members appointed by the Chancellor. The appointment of external members to the Committee is meant to ensure that the Monetary Policy Committee benefits from thinking and expertise in addition to that gained inside the Bank of England. Members serve fixed terms after which they may be replaced or reappointed. The Monetary Policy Committee meets every month to set the interest rate.

The Bank of England is charged with the task of meeting the government's inflation target, which is now 2.0 per cent based on the CPI measure of inflation. The target is symmetrical – inflation below or above the target is viewed as equally undesirable. Inflation will not always be 2.0 per cent. The aim is that it is 2.0 per cent on average over time. The independent nine-member Monetary Policy Committee sets the interest rate each month at a level it believes is consistent with achieving the inflation target.

The Bank of Japan

The Bank of Japan issued its first banknotes on 18 May 1885. In 1897, Japan joined the gold standard and in 1899 the former 'national' banknotes were formally phased out. The Bank of Japan has continued ever since, with the exception of a brief post-World War Two hiatus when the occupying Allies issued military currency and restructured the Bank into a partially independent entity.

The Bank of Japan gained operational independence in April 1998. The Bank is still not legally independent, a status prevented by the Japanese Constitution. In addition, representatives of both the Ministry of Finance and the Economic Planning Agency attend meetings in a non-voting capacity. Before 1998, the Ministry of Finance could require the Bank to delay implementation of a change in policy; now it can only ask. Recently, the Ministry of Finance did indeed ask the policy committee of the Bank of Japan to delay a decision to raise the Bank's target interest rate. In an exercise of the Bank's newly attained power, the policy committee rejected the request and the interest rate increase became effective immediately. This action demonstrated to the public the operational independence of the Bank of Japan. While such an incident is often unfortunate when it happens, it is sometimes a necessary signal to the political authorities to mind their own business and to leave the central bank alone to do its job.

Despite a major 1998 rewrite of the Bank of Japan Law intended to give it more independence, the Bank of Japan has been criticized for lack of independence, particularly because a certain degree of dependence is enshrined in the Law itself, Article 4 of which states: 'In recognition of the fact that currency and monetary control is a component of overall economic policy, the Bank of Japan shall always maintain close contact with the government and exchange views sufficiently, so that its currency and monetary control and the basic stance of the government's economic policy shall be mutually harmonious.'

The European Central Bank

The European Central Bank began operating on 1 June 1998, and assumed responsibility for monetary policy in the euro area on 1 January 1999. The European Central Bank is the world's first supranational central bank[2] and probably qualifies as the most independent central bank in the world. The charter for the European System of Central Banks (ESCB) (composed of the European Central Bank and the national central banks of the member countries) is an international treaty that can be changed

Figure 2.1 The European Central Bank Eurotower in Frankfurt, Germany
Source: ECB website.

only by the unanimous consent of its signatories. With its supranational status, the European Central Bank is further removed from the political pressure of national governments than even the most independent national central banks. In addition, there is no political counterpart to the supranational European Central Bank. The European Parliament carries out oversight hearings on monetary policy but does not have any authority with respect to the European Central Bank.

The Treaty (in Article 107) and the Statute of the ESCB (in Article 7) both contain very clear provisions regarding the relationship with third parties, which leave no room whatsoever for misinterpretation. To quote a key sentence: 'neither the ECB, nor a national central bank, nor any member of their decision-making bodies shall seek or take instructions from Community institutions or bodies, from any government of a Member State or from any other body'. Moreover, the aforementioned

Figure 2.2 The euro: official currency of the European Union countries

authorities shall also 'undertake to respect this principle and not to seek to influence the members of the decision-making bodies of the ECB or of the national central banks in the performance of their tasks'. To put it simply: the door to the single monetary policy is locked from both sides, and neither the ESCB nor third parties can open the door for political instructions. Even an attempt to do so would already be in conflict with the provisions of the Treaty and the Statute of the ESCB.

For national central banks to become an integral part of the ESCB, Member States have to ensure that national legislation is compatible with the Treaty (Article 108) and the Statute of the ESCB (Article 14). This obligation of legal convergence does not require the full harmonization of central bank statutes, but merely insists that inconsistencies with the Treaty be eliminated in respect of features such as institutional, personal, functional and financial independence. This requirement applies to all Member States, including those which may initially be unable to adopt the single currency due to insufficient economic convergence. Exceptions are Denmark and the United Kingdom, which enjoy the right to 'opt in' or 'opt out' of the European Monetary Union (EMU). Member States have made significant progress in recent years in amending their central bank statutes where needed in order to fulfil their Treaty obligations. For example, major reforms have taken place in Belgium, Spain, France, Luxembourg, Portugal, Germany, the Netherlands and Finland.

The importance of these institutional arrangements for creating an appropriate monetary policy setting in stage three of EMU cannot be underestimated. This can be illustrated by reference to the following two arguments. First, these arrangements underline the continuity with the experience of the European Union (EU) central banks with the most successful track record in terms of price stability over the past decades. In fact, in legal terms the ECB enjoys an even higher degree of independence than the most independent national central banks taken separately. Moreover, these legal arrangements are firmly anchored in the Maastricht Treaty and could thus only be changed by a Treaty revision. Without doubt, this is a very difficult and time-consuming procedure, involving both the European Parliament and all the national parliaments, which thus ensures that such a step is not taken lightly. This brings us to the second point, namely that the ECB did not initially have a clear track record of its own, other than the average track record that it may have inherited from the participating national central banks. This implies that financial markets and the general public had initially to assess the performance of the ECB on the basis of the effectiveness of the monetary policy framework adopted and its ability to act in accordance with its primary objective.

Taken together, these two arguments make it clear that the independence of the ESCB underpins the credibility and effectiveness of the single monetary policy and is thus a key condition for the maintenance of price stability in the euro area. Given this legal framework, the Governing Council of the ECB has been able to decide on the basis of its own judgement on the scope and timing of monetary policy actions and how they should be executed. Naturally, in its assessment the Governing Council takes account of a wide range of relevant factors – including the state of the economy in the Monetary Union – but only to the extent that they affect future price developments. This does not imply, as is sometimes suggested, that the secondary objective of providing support to the general economic policies in the community has no real meaning. Nevertheless, under its mandate the ESCB can only pursue this additional goal provided it does not prejudice the primary objective of price stability.

A natural complement to the independent status of the ESCB is the Treaty provisions which make the ECB accountable for its policy actions. Accountability is reflected above all in the fact that the president and the other members of the Executive Board of the ECB, at their own initiative or on request, may be heard by the competent committees of the European Parliament (Article 109b.3). A further aspect of accountability concerns the requirement to publish an annual report covering the single monetary policy and other activities of the ESCB. The president of the ECB presents this annual report to the Council and the European Parliament, which on that basis could subsequently hold a general debate. Reports on the activities of the ESCB are also published during the year, at least quarterly, in addition to weekly financial statements.

All these provisions, in addition to the delivery of speeches to the public and statements to the press, clearly promote the transparency of monetary policy objectives, intentions and actions. They thereby support the effectiveness of monetary policy. At the same time, the Treaty recognizes that the ECB cannot be made responsible for outcomes in terms of inflation month-by-month, since there are lags involved between a change in the course of monetary policy and its effect on prices. Moreover, in the short term, the inflation outcome may reflect the incidence of temporary or external factors over which the ECB has no control.

At this point, critical observers often confront the ECB with the fact that the door is not completely shut against political interference, as the Treaty seems to make an exception to the independence of the ESCB with regard to the exchange rate policy of the euro area. The Economic and Financial Council (ECOFIN) may indeed conclude formal exchange rate arrangements with countries outside the EU, or formulate general orientations for exchange rate policy in relation to the currencies of these non-EU countries. This essentially reflects the current situation in most Member States, where the government determines the exchange rate rules (if any) and the central bank is responsible for the execution of this policy. On closer inspection, however, there should be no fear of a potential overburdening of the single monetary policy via this route.

To begin with, the participation of the euro in a multinational system with non-EU currencies is, to say the least, not on the agenda. And as regards the 'general orientations for exchange rate policy', while such orientations are indeed in the hands of ECOFIN, they can be issued only either on a recommendation from the ECB or on a recommendation from the Commission – but after consulting the ECB. And Article 109 of the Treaty says explicitly that 'these general orientations shall be without prejudice to the primary objective of the ESCB to maintain price stability'.

Overall, it appears that sufficient 'checks and balances' have been built into the procedure. The view of the ECB in these exchange rate matters carries a very high weight indeed and the independence of the ESCB is not affected. That this is the case also finds support in the fact that the European Monetary Institute (EMI) has played a crucial role in helping to design the new exchange rate mechanism (ERM II) for establishing links between the euro and the non-participating EU currencies. To everyone's satisfaction, the arrangement contains an explicit safeguard clause for the ECB (and other central banks) with regard to automatic intervention and financing at the margin, and also assigns a key role to the

ECB (and other central banks) in negotiations that may culminate in realignments.

So far, I have mainly concentrated on the two 'monetary anchors' that help to provide for a stable single currency: the objective of price stability and the mandate for an independent monetary policy. But we all know that other economic policies have an essential supporting role to play in the effort to maintain price stability on a durable basis. In this respect, ensuring sound and sustainable budgetary positions does certainly make the ESCB's task a lot easier. Fortunately, a series of Treaty provisions support a high degree of fiscal discipline – which is of course also very much in the interests of Member States themselves. Already, Member States have no longer been allowed to engage in monetary financing of budget deficits (Article 104). Correspondingly, it is explicitly forbidden for the ESCB to supply credit facilities to government bodies, or to buy government debt instruments in the primary market.

In addition, financial institutions are not allowed to grant credit to public authorities under preferential conditions (Article 104a). Furthermore, a bail-out of one Member State with financial problems by another country is strictly excluded (Article 104b). Finally, the Treaty obliges EU countries participating in the single currency to avoid excessive budget deficits (Article 104c). Compliance with this obligation is assessed in the context of an elaborate procedure which ultimately leads to the imposition of sanctions if no effective action is taken to correct an excessive deficit. The preventive nature and effectiveness of this procedure have recently been strengthened by the adoption of a Stability and Growth Pact, which specifies both the time limits for the consecutive steps in the procedure and the size of sanctions. Moreover, it commits each Member State to target a budgetary position that is close to balance or in surplus over the medium term. The *Financial Times* noted in September 2007 that during his press conference, Mr Jean Claude Trichet, President of the European Central Bank, reacted angrily to suggestions that the ECB failed to raise rates as a result of pressures from Mr Nicholas Sarkozy, President of France, who was quoted as saying: 'It demonstrates that our efforts to talk about interest rates and raise the issue are yielding some small results.' Mr Trichet responded immediately by saying that the bank was 'fiercely independent', and that the interest rate decision was derived from the ECB's own analysis. On 24 December 2007, the *Financial Times* selected Mr Trichet as its man of the year for his handling of the banking liquidity crisis in the eurozone following the speculative attacks on the euro and American dollars as the result of the subprime mortgage[3] defaults in the United States and Europe. In particular, Mr Trichet was lauded for his rapid reaction in handling the crisis while asserting the independence of the European Central Bank vis-à-vis the European governments and also the US Federal Reserve System. Again, as in the case of the Bank of Japan, these small fights between the central bank and the government are necessary to ascertain and anchor the independence of the monetary authority in public opinion.

The Swiss National Bank

Switzerland is a small country with a land size area of 41,285 square kilometres and a population of 7.5 million, but enjoys a strong currency and a vibrant financial system, thanks to its highly credible central bank and its sound economic, financial and fiscal policies. The central bank of the Swiss Confederation is the Swiss National Bank, which started business in 1907. It deals mainly with commercial and investment banks, acting as the bank of banks, and with various Federal agencies, in its capacity as the Confederation's bank. The Swiss National Bank's chief function, according to Article 39 of the Federal Constitution, is to regulate the country's money circulation, to facilitate payment transactions and to pursue a credit and monetary policy serving the interests of the country as a whole. This formulation also appears in the Swiss National Bank Law. The article of the Federal Constitution providing for the regulation of economic activity, introduced only in 1978, defines the aims of the Confederation's counter-cyclical policy as balanced development of economic activity, especially the prevention and combating of unemployment and inflation.

Price level stability is important particularly because (relative) prices in the market-economy system govern the production and consumption of individual goods. Changes in the price level may give misleading signals and lead to expensive mistakes in planning and investments. For the Swiss National Bank, the prevention and combating of inflation is of special significance, because protracted changes in the price level are, as a rule, due to a malfunctioning of the monetary system.

Monetary policy in Switzerland

Initial system of fixed exchange rates. Until the beginning of the 1970s, fixed exchange rates existed, in principle, between most currencies – in earlier years by virtue of the gold standard and after World War Two by virtue of the gold exchange standard in accordance with the rules of the International Monetary Fund. The central bank of a country had to regulate the money supply in such a way as to ensure that the exchange rate of the country's own currency remained constant in relation to gold or

Figure 2.3 The Swiss National Bank headquarters in Berne

to the key currency, usually the US dollar. This system helped to maintain fixed exchange rates and facilitated the international exchange of goods. At the same time, inflation and deflation tended to be transferred internationally under this system without any individual country being able to protect itself adequately against these effects.

Move towards autonomous monetary policies. When, in 1971, the United States put an end to the convertibility of the dollar into gold, the pressure of inflation led to a collapse of the system of fixed exchange rates within less than two years. The abolition of fixed exchange rates afforded the Swiss National Bank the possibility of steering the money supply in accordance with the needs of the Swiss economy. It acted on the assumption that, at least in the longer term, there is a close correlation between the money supply and the development of the price level. Accelerated expansion of the money supply as a rule leads to a rise in inflation, while a contraction in the growth of the money supply has the effect of curbing inflation. The price level does not, however, react immediately to changes in the money supply; the time lag is considerable and is estimated to be two to three years.

Money supply targets as a guideline. Since the exchange rate constraint has been lifted, the Swiss National Bank has been orienting its policy to money supply targets. In this way, it not only creates a framework for its own activity in the money and financial markets, but also provides a guideline to the public, thus taking account of the fact that economic development is considerably influenced by the expectations of enterprises and households. Initially the money supply target was fixed at the end of every year for the following year. In the first few years, it was oriented to the money supply M (defined as notes and coins in circulation plus deposits of domestic non-banks at banks and on postal checking accounts) and later to the monetary base (notes in circulation plus the banks' sight deposits at the Swiss National Bank). At the end of 1990, the Swiss National Bank abandoned its practice of fixing a money supply target for the following calendar year. Nevertheless, it continues to aim at a money supply growth that will guarantee a stable price level. Based on the Swiss National Bank studies, this should be achieved when, in the medium-term average, the monetary base expands by approximately 1 per cent per year. In addition, the Swiss National Bank keeps the markets and the public informed of its short-term monetary policy by announcing every quarter how it expects the monetary base to develop in the course of the following three months.

Technically, the Swiss National Bank can expand (or contract) the monetary base at virtually any time and to any desired degree by purchasing (or selling) domestic or foreign assets and by granting (or reducing the volume of) credits. If, in actual practice, the Swiss National Bank has not always achieved its monetary targets, this is due to the fact that it has been willing to accept deviations from the original targets in the case of external disruptions. Thus the Swiss National Bank has repeatedly reacted to extreme exchange rate fluctuations or to a changing demand for liquidity. A case in point is the massive expansion in the supply of money in autumn 1978, when the Swiss franc threatened to soar far beyond an economically justifiable level. Another example is the reduction in the supply of money in 1988 and 1989, when the banks' demand for sight deposits fell markedly due to the changed liquidity requirements and the introduction of the electronic system for interbank payments, Swiss Interbank Clearing.

Consideration of exchange rates and employment in case of serious disruptions

The Swiss National Bank assumes that a short-term monetary policy presupposes a certain degree of flexibility. Rigidly adhering to money supply targets could well lead to undesirable exchange rate volatility in Switzerland, which is a small country with a strong international involvement. However, considerable restraint is required to smooth such fluctuations. Not every change in the exchange rate calls for an adjustment of monetary policy. This depends on the factors that trigger the exchange rate change in a specific case. Since it is frequently not possible to determine these factors and to quantify their effects early enough, the Swiss National Bank often refrains from reacting to minor disruptions. On the contrary, it reserves deviations from the envisaged money supply expansion for special situations. Otherwise the result is a policy oriented to the very short term which would eventually lead to less, rather than more, stability.

The Swiss National Bank's instruments for controlling the monetary base

The Swiss National Bank influences the development of the monetary base by buying or selling assets or by granting or not renewing credits. The operations that the Swiss National Bank is allowed to carry out in order to influence the monetary base are enumerated in the Swiss National Bank Law, and include the following: (i) the purchase and sale of foreign currencies; (ii) the conclusion of foreign-currency swaps; (iii) open market operations in money market debt register claims; (iv) the purchase and sale of securities; and (v) the granting of advances against securities (Lombard advances).

In the case of the first four of the above-mentioned possibilities, the initiative for carrying out a transaction lies with the Swiss National Bank; in the case of lending against securities, the Swiss National Bank fixes the terms and leaves the initiative to the commercial banks. The kind of transactions the Swiss National Bank carries out in order to achieve its objectives is of secondary importance from the point of view of monetary policy. What is more crucial for the influence it has on inflation, exchange rates and the level of interest rates is the development of the money supply.

Independence within the government

The Swiss National Bank is an independent institution and is obliged by the Constitution and statute to direct its actions towards the interest of the Swiss economy. Since the Swiss National Bank has a responsibility towards the public, the federal government is involved in its administration.

In order to realize its objectives, the Swiss National Bank undertakes the following functions: (i) issuing and controlling the circulation of banknotes in the country; (ii) ensuring price stability in the country; (iii) carrying out banking transactions on behalf of the Swiss Confederation; and (iv) advising the central government on financial and economic matters.

The bank has a considerable degree of independence in carrying out its functions. However, at the same time the Swiss National Bank is required to report regularly to the Federal Council and the public at large on the developments concerning monetary policy. The Swiss National Bank's monetary policy influences the economy in numerous ways. The monetary policy influences the exchange rate and the interest rates, and thus the level of inflation.

The administration of the Swiss National Bank is in the hands of three departments. While Department I has the responsibility of preparing the monetary policy, Department II is responsible for issuing the banknotes and carrying out banking transactions on behalf of the Swiss Confederation. Department II is also responsible for monitoring the developments in the financial system. Department III is concerned with implementing the monetary policy and conducting foreign currency transactions.

In sum, the Swiss National Bank serves as the country's central bank. Its shares are publicly traded and are held by the cantons, cantonal banks and individual investors; the federal government does not hold any shares. Although a central bank often has regulatory authority over the country's banking system, the Swiss National Bank does not; regulation is solely in the hands of the Federal Banking Commission.

The Federal Reserve System

The Federal Reserve, created in 1913, was established as an independent central bank – although, at the time, it was given no clear concept of its role in the conduct of monetary policy. The only reference to policy goals in the original Federal Reserve Act was that the Federal Reserve of the United States was responsible for providing an elastic currency, i.e. one that would expand as appropriate to accommodate the need for additional transactions as production and spending grew.

The major question for the founders was the degree to which the American central bank should be a public or a private institution. Bankers wanted a largely private central bank. Populists wanted a public institution. President Wilson and Congressman Glass steered a middle course. There would be a Federal Reserve Board that was completely public, and the Federal Reserve banks would have significant characteristics of private institutions. During the first fifty years of the Federal Reserve Bank's history, Congress continued to focus more on issues involving the structure of the Federal Reserve than on providing a clear legislative mandate for monetary policy or oversight of the conduct of monetary policy.

A former Fed governor, Andrew Brimmer, in a 1989 speech entitled 'Politics and Monetary Policy: Presidential Efforts to Control the Federal Reserve', describes the record of almost 'continuous and at least public and vigorous conflicts' between presidents and the Federal Reserve. In his view, twelve of the fourteen presidents between the founding of the Federal Reserve and the time he was writing – from Woodrow Wilson to George Bush – had 'some kind of public debate, conflict, or criticism of the Federal Reserve monetary policy', the exceptions being Calvin Coolidge and Gerald Ford. He alleged that presidents resented the delegation of monetary policy by the Congress to an independent Federal Reserve and sought ways to bring monetary policy under their influence, often by exerting direct political pressure on the Federal Reserve, but principally through the appointment process. Examples of the latter cited by Brimmer include: Richard Nixon, who believed that the Federal Reserve had cost him the election in 1960 and replaced Chairman William McChesney Martin with Arthur Burns in February 1970 when Martin's term expired; Jimmy Carter, who appointed William Miller to replace Chairman Burns in 1978; and Ronald Reagan, who appointed Alan Greenspan as Chairman in 1987. After losing the election to Bill Clinton, George Bush senior said bluntly of Alan Greenspan: 'I reappointed him and he disappointed me'.[4] For the most part, their best efforts to appoint sympathetic choices as Chairmen have, in Brimmer's judgement, been frustrated by the systematic tendency of Chairmen and other board members to insist on exercising their Congressional mandate.

Thomas M. Havrilesky (1992) also provides an account of, and some attempts to measure, the intensity of political pressure over time, based on the number of comments on monetary policy made by administration officials, including the president, and by members of Congress. He concludes that there was little pressure from the executive branch during the Eisenhower and Ford administrations, but many more such efforts in the Kennedy, Johnson and Nixon administrations. In addition to this assessment made by Havrilesky, the number of comments on monetary policy made by administration officials also intensified during George Bush senior's term of office, while Bill Clinton and Treasury Secretary Robert Rubin co-opted Alan Greenspan to such an extent that the barrier between the Federal Reserve and the administration became blurred. But this closeness between Alan Greenspan, Robert Rubin and Bill Clinton was much more a reflection of agreement on policies and vision than a

Figure 2.4 The Federal Reserve building in Washington, D.C.

compromise of central bank independence. It also means that independence goes way beyond what is written on paper and cannot be used as a justification for lack of friendly and sincere collaboration between the central bank and the executive branch of the government. Competent people tend to find ways to work together for a common agenda as they pursue well-understood objectives individually and collectively.

The Clinton administration respected the independence of the Federal Reserve to a degree that, given the accounts of others, may exceed that of any previous administration. To be sure, President Clinton had opportunities to make appointments to the Federal Reserve Board and he twice reappointed Alan Greenspan as Chairman. But the administration never made any public or private effort to influence monetary policy.

The Federal Reserve has been technically independent of the president from the beginning, even though the Secretary of the Treasury and the Comptroller of the Currency originally sat on the board. Although it is a creature of the Congress, the Federal Reserve Act delegated control over the currency to the board and Congress insulated the Federal Reserve from elective politics to a large degree. The current structure of the Federal Open Market Committee (FOMC) was introduced in the Banking Act of 1935, which became effective in March 1936. At that time the Secretary of the Treasury and the Comptroller of the Currency

Figure 2.5 The US dollar: official currency of the USA

were removed from the board. The terms of governors were extended from ten to fourteen years and the Chairman and Vice-Chairman were made appointees from within the board with four-year terms. This structural change is often viewed as allowing the culture of independence to flourish at the Fed.

The legislation was also a battle between the administration and Congress. The administration wanted to shift the power over monetary policy towards the centralized and presidentially appointed Federal Reserve Board governors, a group they had a better opportunity to influence through the appointment process. Congress partly resisted and partly diluted the control of the administration by allowing a role for the Reserve Bank's presidents on the FOMC.

During both world wars, the US Treasury wanted to issue securities at low interest rates to ease the burden of financing and the Fed went along with this plan because it felt bound to facilitate wartime financing. In addition, during World War One, Reserve banks bought most of the government's first $50 million certificate issue directly from the Treasury despite strong objections from some System officials. Such direct purchases were later eliminated and the statutory prohibition on direct underwriting of government debt is today considered one of the principal protections of the independence of a central bank. After World War One, the Treasury opposed raising the discount rate to combat inflation, but the Fed did so anyway.

During World War Two, the Fed sacrificed its independence by agreeing to peg the Treasury yield curve to ensure low rates for wartime financing. After the war, the Fed wanted to resume an independent monetary policy, fearing that it would otherwise become an engine of inflation, but the Treasury was still concerned about minimizing the service cost of the debt. To resolve this conflict, an agreement was negotiated in 1951 by Assistant Secretary of the Treasury William McChesney Martin and Fed officials. The Congress, led by Senator Paul Douglas, also played an important role through its support for the Federal Reserve's independence. Under the terms of the Accord, as it came to be known, the Fed was no longer obligated to peg the interest rates on Treasury debt, but it was agreed that active consultation between the Fed and the Treasury would continue. That active consultation continues today.

From the end of World War Two until the mid-1970s, the mandate for monetary policy was based on the Employment Act of 1946. This legislation set out a general mandate for the government. Although it did not explicitly refer to the Federal Reserve, it was widely understood that the Act applied to the central bank as a part of government. The Act identified the government's macroeconomic policy objectives as fostering 'conditions under which there will be useful employment opportunities for those able, willing, and seeking to work, and to promote maximum employment, production, and purchasing power'.

Conflict between the executive branch and the Federal Reserve erupted dramatically in December 1965. President Johnson did not want the administration's stimulative fiscal policy undermined by restrictive monetary policy. Chairman Martin supported an increase in the discount rate as an appropriate step to contain the risk of higher inflation. A key vote occurred on a proposed increase in the discount rate at a board meeting on 3 December. Although the president tried to influence the Chairman's position, and others in the administration put pressure on other members of the board, the Board of Governors voted 4–3 to support the Chairman. Following the vote, the president summoned the Chairman to his ranch in Texas. But the vote stood. The independence of the Fed was preserved and indeed used for precisely the purpose it was intended. Subsequently, virtually everyone agreed it had been the correct decision. The system worked.

Congress became more involved in the monetary policy process in the 1970s. This was a response to both poor economic performance and changing views about the importance of monetary aggregates in shaping economic developments, especially inflation. Inflation began to rise in the late 1960s and escalated further in the 1970s. During this period, monetarism was an increasing influence, with its focus on the importance of limiting the rate of growth of the money supply to control inflation. But it was the sharp recession in 1974–5 that really provoked

Congress to provide more detailed instructions to the Federal Reserve about the objectives that should guide monetary policy.

In 1975, the House and Senate passed Concurrent Resolution 133 calling on the Fed to lower long-term interest rates and expand the monetary and credit aggregates to promote recovery. The Fed was also instructed to set money growth targets and to participate in periodic Congressional hearings on monetary policy. For the first time, Congress explicitly identified the objectives for monetary policy. The same language about the objectives applies today. Still, with its focus on the conduct of monetary policy at a point in time (rather than on general guidelines on policy objectives to be applied over time), the resolution was a clear instance of action by Congress to intervene and influence monetary policy.

The monetary policy objectives written into the Concurrent Resolution were added by an amendment to the Federal Reserve Act in 1977 and were further elaborated in the Full Employment and Balanced Growth Act of 1978, often referred to as the Humphrey–Hawkins Act after its co-sponsors.

Another clear attempt at political interference emerged in February 1988 when an undersecretary of the Treasury sent a letter to Federal Reserve officials urging them to ease monetary policy. The request was promptly and publicly rebuked by Chairman Greenspan. Having an attempt at political pressure become public and be sharply rejected was an unusual event in the history of the relationship between the executive branch and the Federal Reserve.

The reporting requirements in the Humphrey–Hawkins Act expired in May 2000. As a result, Congress is now reconsidering the monetary policy oversight process. In part because the link between money growth and nominal spending appears to be less tight than it was earlier, the role of money growth in monetary policy deliberations has diminished and it appears likely that Congress will no longer require the Fed to set and report money growth ranges. However, the current language about the objectives of monetary policy seems likely to be retained, as does a semi-annual testimony on monetary policy.

The Central Bank of the Congo

The above historical perspective is important in helping the Congolese executive and legislative branches as well as the public to get a clear sense of the evolution of the concept of central bank independence in other countries. This knowledge can be useful for understanding some of the policy stances that a central bank in an emerging economy may need to

Figure 2.6 The Banque Centrale du Congo in Kinshasa
Source: www.lesoftonline.net (reproduced with kind permission from the Hon. Tryphon Kin-kiey Mulumba, owner and managing director of Le Soft International).

take in a deliberate effort to build credibility under a new leadership or beyond.

The Central Bank of the Congo has gone through various cycles since its inception in 1961. The statutes of the central bank have never been taken seriously in terms of maintaining a strict independence from the executive branch of the government. Under the first and second republics, the tradition in the Congo has been one of a central bank that is totally obedient and subservient to the executive branch. The lack of independence has been very clear through the very high turnover of central bank governors and vice-governors and the presence of government ministers on the board of the central bank. It was only in 2002 that the transitional Parliament passed for the first time in the history of the country a specific law (Law no. 005/2002, 7 May 2002, relating to the constitution, organization and functioning of the Central Bank of the Congo) granting independence to the Central Bank of the Congo. While the law is a positive step forward, it is still imperfect and will need further fine-tuning in order to insulate the monetary policy from continued political interference. In particular, the composition of the board of the central bank needs rethinking as well as the requirement for clearer accountability and transparency in central bank management. Also, the bank must be made clearly responsible for monetary stability. Monetary stability means stable prices – low inflation – and confidence in the currency. Stable prices will need to be defined by the government's inflation target, which the bank will seek to meet through the decisions on

Figure 2.7 The Congolese franc: official currency of the Democratic Republic of the Congo

interest rates taken by the proposed Monetary Policy Committee or the National Open Market Committee.The size of the government's deficit and the methods by which it is financed determine central bank independence in the Democratic Republic of the Congo. In the Congo, a good measure of the central bank's independence is the extent to which the BCC neutralizes the effects of increased credit demands by the government on the money supply by reducing credit to the private sector. Larger deficits and greater government reliance on the domestic banking system are associated with less central bank neutralization of increased government borrowing from the banking system. The monetary authorities have to make themselves available to work closely with both the Senate and the National Assembly to move forward the central bank independence agenda to greater heights.

The hallmark of good central banking is the maintenance of low levels of inflation over extended periods. But what institutional structure is most likely to achieve and preserve low inflation? Central banks are considered more independent when they can resist the pressure to make short-term policy decisions that are at odds with their long-term objectives. Central banks gain independence chiefly through institutional reforms such as long-term appointments for central bank governors, explicit inflation targets, and a combination of institutional reforms and targeting. The element common to both inflation targeting and central bank independence is constraint of the fiscal authority's behaviour.

At first glance, it is hard to see any benefit in imposing constraint on oneself. But most of us need some sort of discipline or commitment in the face of temptation, whether it is in the form of Ulysses having himself lashed to the mast to resist the lure of the Sirens, or moving the alarm clock to the far side of the bedroom to withstand the desire for extra sleep. Such constraints inhibit people from acting in their short-term interest, recognizing that actions that seem optimal in the short term may be undesirable in the long term. The same is true of the fiscal authority, which may be tempted to inflate in the short run to deliver, say, a more favourable exchange rate, a higher output rate, or a lower level of inflation-adjusted debt. These short-run temptations may contravene the goal of long-run price stability, and it may therefore be in society's best interest to grant monetary policy power to an independent, far-sighted central bank headed by an independent central bank person. In the context of the Democratic Republic of the Congo, independence of the central bank can be promoted with the appointment of a governor who is not from the same province or the same political party as the president of the Republic, the prime minister, the minister of finance, the minister of budget, the president of the National Assembly or the president of the Senate. Above all, the appointment criteria must include technical competence, and vision for the central bank, the financial sector and the currency.

Professionalizing the monetary policy process in the Congo

Under the current system, the Board of Directors of the Central Bank of the Congo approves policy instruments proposed by bank management. The board is made up of a mix of personalities, some of whom lack the appropriate technical expertise to take policy decisions such as the level of interest rates and reserve requirements. It is with this in mind that I propose the creation of a technical body to take decisions on monetary policy. While waiting for the move towards a decentralized system of central banking where monetary policy decisions would be delegated to the National Open Market Committee, I propose under the current centralized structure of the Central Bank of the Congo, the establishment of a Monetary Policy Committee (MPC) which would set interest rates, mandatory reserves on deposits, and other policy instruments.

Composition of the Monetary Policy Committee

The MPC would set an interest rate it judges will enable the inflation target to be met. The MPC could be made up of twelve members – the seven board members plus five persons appointed by the president on the basis of their technical expertise. The MPC would in particular include, among others, the Governor, the Deputy Governor, the Bank's Chief Economist, the Director for Markets, the Director for Research, all the board members and external members appointed directly by the president of the Republic and approved by the Senate. The appointment of external members would be designed to ensure that the MPC benefits from thinking and expertise from outside the Central Bank of the Congo. Members would serve fixed three-year terms after which they would be replaced or reappointed.

Each member of the MPC would have expertise in the field of economics, business, banking, finance, and monetary policy. Members would not represent individual groups or areas. They would be independent. Each member of the Committee would have a vote to set interest rates at the level they believe is consistent with meeting the inflation target. The MPC's decision would be made on the basis of one-person, one vote. It would not be based on a consensus of opinion. It would reflect the votes of each individual member of the Committee.

A representative from the Ministry of Finance would also sit with the Committee at its meetings. The Ministry of Finance representative could discuss policy issues but would not be allowed to vote. The purpose of this would be to ensure that the MPC is fully briefed on fiscal policy developments and other aspects of the government's economic policies, and that the president of the Republic is kept fully informed about monetary policy.

MPC meetings

The MPC could meet every month to set the interest rate. Throughout the month, the MPC could receive extensive briefing on the economy from the Central Bank of the Congo staff. This would include a half-day meeting – to be known as the pre-MPC meeting – which could take place on the Friday before the MPC's interest rate setting meeting. The members of the Committee would be made aware of all the latest data on the economy and hear explanations of recent trends and analysis of relevant issues. The Committee would also be told about business conditions around the Congo from the bank's staff. The staff's role is to talk directly to business to gain intelligence and insight into current and future economic developments and prospects.

The monthly MPC meeting itself would be a two-day affair. On the first day, the meeting could start with an update on the most recent economic data gathered by the Central Bank. A series of issues would then be identified for discussion. On the following day, a summary of the previous day's discussion could be provided and the MPC members individually would explain their views on what policy should be. The Central Bank governor then would put to the meeting the policy which he believes would command a majority and members of the MPC would then vote. The governor would chair the MPC meeting and would have an original and the casting vote. The governor would be the last to cast his vote, which effectively would act as a casting vote in the event of a tie. Any member in a minority would be asked to say what level of interest rates he or she would have preferred, and this would be recorded in the minutes of the meeting. The interest rate decision would be announced at 12:00 noon on the second day.

Explaining views and decisions

The MPC would go to great lengths to explain its thinking and decisions. The minutes of the MPC meetings would be published two weeks after the interest rate decision. The minutes would give a full account of the policy discussion, including differences of view. They would also record the votes of the individual members of the Committee. The Committee would explain its actions regularly to parliamentary committees, particularly the National Assembly and Senate Finance Committees. MPC members would also speak[5] to audiences throughout the country, explaining the MPC's policy decisions and thinking. This would be a two-way dialogue. Provincial visits would also give members of the MPC a chance to gather first-hand intelligence about the economic situation from businesses and other organizations.

In addition to the monthly MPC minutes, the Central Bank of the Congo would publish its Inflation Report every quarter. This report would give an analysis of the Congolese economy and the factors influencing policy decisions. The Inflation Report would also include the MPC's latest forecasts for inflation and output growth. Because monetary policy operates with a time lag of about two years, it would be necessary for the MPC to form judgements about the outlook for output and inflation. The MPC would use sophisticated economic models to help produce its projections. The model would provide a framework to organize thinking on how the economy works and how different economic developments might affect future inflation. But this is not a mechanical exercise. Given all the uncertainties and unknowns of the future, the MPC's forecast would have to involve a great deal of judgement about the economy.

Focus on the stability of the financial system

One of the BCC's core purposes is to maintain the stability of the financial system. The Central Bank of the Congo has to make sure that the overall system is safe and secure and that threats to financial stability are detected and reduced. By monitoring and analysing the behaviour of participants in the financial system and the wider financial and economic environment, the Central Bank of the Congo aims to identify potential vulnerabilities and risks, with a view to making the system stronger. The Bank's role includes oversight of payment systems – a crucial part of the financial system, which facilitates transactions between individuals, businesses and financial institutions. To broaden the scope of the central bank mission, there is a need to adjust the mandate of the Central Bank of the Congo to move from price stability to financial stability which would include price stability, the stability of the financial system and the promotion of confidence in the value of the currency.

Board of Directors of the BCC

The Central Bank of the Congo has a Board of Directors whose primary function should be expanded to include the responsibility to review the performance of the Governor and of the Bank. The board, which meets now at very irregular times, should hold regular meetings at which it would receive extensive briefings on the Bank's activities, decisions and policies. At these meetings the board would also provide advice to the governor. The distinction between the MPC and the board is that the former would specialize and focus on monetary policy issues, while the latter would have an overall broad mandate on the central bank's management.

The primary responsibility of the board members is the formulation of monetary policy. The board members would constitute a majority of the twelve-member MPC (or later the National Open Market Committee (NOMC)), the group that makes the key decisions affecting the cost and availability of money and credit in the economy. The other five members of the MPC or NOMC would represent the regional financial districts. By statute the MPC or NOMC would determine its own organization, and by tradition it would be required to elect the governor as its chairman and a representative of a regional financial district as its vice-chairman.

The board, through an Audit Committee, should also review the bank's financial statements. Each year, the board would have to write an assessment of the bank's and the governor's performance, which would be provided as advice to the minister of finance and made public later in the bank's Annual Report.

Where does a central bank get its independence from?

Central bank independence is in part the result of formal institutional features typically incorporated in the legislation creating and defining the central bank. The legislation creating an 'independent' central bank – or in many cases revisions to such legislation – often takes away goal independence entirely by mandating objectives for monetary policy, but otherwise sets up a structure that confers and protects instrument independence. The most important requirement for instrument independence is for the central bank to be the final authority on monetary policy. That is, monetary policy decisions should not be subject to veto by the executive or legislative branches of government. Instrument independence is further protected if other institutions of government are not represented on the Monetary Policy Committee. A lesser protection would be to allow government representation but only in a non-voting capacity.

Instrument independence is further facilitated by long, overlapping terms for members of the Monetary Policy Committee; by limited opportunities for reappointment; and by committee members not being subject to removal except for cause – where 'cause' refers to fraud or other personal misconduct but explicitly excludes differences in judgement about policy. An intangible contributor to independence, but arguably the most important, is the appointment of a capable, respected, politically astute, and 'independent-minded' Governor.

A third important protection of independence is achieved by freeing the central bank from the appropriations process. Many central banks have been granted the seignorage function – issuing currency for the government – and cover the cost of their operations from the earnings on their portfolio of government securities acquired in the process, returning the excess to the government.

Finally, it is critically important to ensure that the central bank is not required to directly underwrite government debt. The Finance Ministry would have an incentive to keep interest rates low to reduce the cost of servicing the government debt. Indeed, perhaps the first principle of central bank independence is independence from the fiscal authority.

If independence is also defined in terms of assuring the ability and commitment of the central bank to achieve price stability, this commitment can be protected by an explicit price stability mandate from the government. That is, a government that explicitly imposes this mandate is less likely to interfere in a central bank's pursuit of this objective. Independence, by this definition, is viewed as greatest if price stability is the exclusive objective of monetary policy, or at least the principal objective.

Academic research on the independence of central banks

Research and analyses of the economic consequences of central bank independence typically estimate the economic effects by first deriving quantitative measures of the relative independence of central banks and then estimating how this measure is correlated with average inflation, inflation variability, and real economic performance. Reviewing three of these studies would help to elucidate the meaning and sources of central bank independence and perhaps provide at least some insights into how the Central Bank of the Congo ranks relative to other central banks in terms of independence.

Bade and Parkin (1988) ranked the political independence of twelve industrial country central banks on the basis of answers to questions such as the following: Is the bank the final policy authority? Is there any government official (with or without voting power) on the bank board? Grilli et al. (1991) also incorporated information on the length of terms of Monetary Policy Committee members and on policy goals of the central bank with respect to monetary policy, specifically whether there is a mandate for monetary stability (including money growth or price stability objectives). Cukierman (1992) also takes into account restrictions on the ability of the public sector to borrow from the central bank. A central bank is more independent if it is protected, for example, from directly underwriting the government debt.

Germany (prior to its participation as part of the European Central Bank) and Switzerland have been uniformly ranked as the most independent of central banks. The US fell into the second tier in Bade and Parkin's rankings; was just below the most independent central banks in Grilli et al.'s rankings of eighteen industrial countries; and was tied for fourth place among seventy countries in Cukierman's rankings. The Federal Reserve lost points in these rankings because of the brevity of the Chairman's term of office (less than five years) and the failure to single out price stability as the unique or principal objective. The Central Bank of the Congo was not included in these rankings. But applying the same criteria to the Central Bank of the Congo, I found, in my doctoral dissertation in 2002 at the Université de Paris IX Dauphine, that our central bank was totally dependent on the executive branch and was subject to a great deal of political interference. My subsequent publications on the issue led, I believe, to the debate that created conditions for the adoption by Parliament of Law no. 005/2002 mentioned above.

Of these studies, I prefer Bade and Parkin's methodology for ranking independence because they included only those institutional characteristics that afforded a measure of independence to the central bank. Grilli et al. and Cukierman also included in their measures the nature of monetary policy objectives, ranking independence higher if there is a price stability objective and, in Cukierman's case, higher still if price stability is the only or at least principal objective. In the latter case, a central bank with more discretion – for example, as a result of multiple objectives – is ranked as less independent than a central bank that has little discretion on account of a single, precisely defined price stability objective. Of course, defining independence to involve a mandate making price stability the single or principal objective increases the potential for an inverse relationship between 'independence' and inflation.

Central bank accountability

Accountability means being answerable for one's decisions. Implicit in being accountable is being subject to discipline for failure to live up to your responsibilities. Making the central bank accountable in this way involves, by definition, some compromise of the independence of the central bank. But accountability is the critical mechanism for ensuring both that the central bank operates in a way consistent with democratic ideals and that the central bank operates under incentives to meet its legislative mandate for monetary policy. On the other hand, steps to increase accountability also create opportunities for political interference.

Every organization's performance is likely to be enhanced by appropriate incentives. In the private sector, the incentives for a business are profitability and, indeed, survival. In the public sector, other means must be found to provide incentives. Elections, of course, play this role for elected officials. With central banks having been given an arm's length relationship from the electoral process (e.g. in New Zealand), some have suggested that central bank policy-makers should operate under explicit incentive contracts. But, for the most part, accountability is achieved for central banks both through the appointment process and by regular oversight by the legislature.

Accountability is facilitated by providing the central bank with a specific, external (usually legislatively imposed) mandate. Two aspects of designing the objectives for monetary policy are important. First, a single objective (typically price stability) makes the central bank more accountable, because multiple targets always carry trade-offs, at least in the short run, which are subject to the discretion of the central bank. Second, explicit numerical targets make central banks more accountable than more general targets. Specifically, an explicit numerical inflation target makes the central bank more accountable than a more general commitment to price stability.

There are, however, other considerations that are relevant to setting the mandate. First, if there is a single target for a central bank, it would surely be price stability, given that monetary policy is the principal, even unique, determinant of inflation in the long run. While a single target is more precise, few legislatures would tolerate a central bank disclaiming any responsibility for the cyclical state of the economy or at least failing to respond to cyclical weakness. Indeed, given the inescapable trade-off between inflation variability and output variability, a central bank naturally, even inevitably, accounts for the variability of output around full employment when deciding how rapidly to try to restore price stability in cases where shocks or policy mistakes move the economy away from this goal. Inflation-targeting central banks often take account of output variability by defining a period of time over which any return to price stability should occur, typically two years. But such a fixed boundary may not encompass the optimal response to all shocks.

A second consideration in setting the mandate is that flexibility can be a valuable asset for policy-makers, given the variety of shocks that the economy may face, structural changes that could affect the nature of trade-offs faced by policy-makers, and the possibility of short-run trade-offs among multiple targets. So, less precise objectives and multiple targets provide flexibility for the policy-maker. To the extent that there is a single and explicit target, accountability is narrowly about performance relative to that target. On the other hand, when there are multiple targets and hence inherent shorter-run flexibility and less precisely defined targets, the oversight by the legislature would typically focus more broadly on the judgements that the central bank has made in pursuing its legislative mandate.

A second source of accountability is through the reappointment process. If terms are short (five years or less) and especially if the governor and other voting members can be reappointed for additional terms, more control can be exercised through the appointment process, and committee members can more easily be held accountable for their policy votes. This is a clear example of the trade-off between independence (facilitated by long terms without the possibility of reappointment) and accountability (facilitated by short terms with opportunities for reappointment).

As noted earlier, Federal Reserve board governors are appointed by the president, subject to Senate confirmation, for nominal fourteen-year terms. Such long, overlapping terms facilitate independence. However, if a board member resigns before his or her term has expired, the successor is appointed for the remainder of that term. At the end of a partial term, a governor can be reappointed for a full term, but reappointment is at the discretion of the president and is again subject to confirmation by the Senate. Once a full term has been served, no reappointment is possible. I would very strongly suggest that the Parliament of the Democratic Republic of the Congo adjust the current central bank law to integrate this best practice experience.

However, the current length of term for the chairman and the vice-chairman of the Board of Governors is only four years and both can be reappointed for additional terms for as long as they remain on the board. Such short and renewable terms reduce independence but facilitate accountability. In addition, they provide an important opportunity for the president to try to influence monetary policy decisions by pressures exerted on the chairman subsequent to appointment. To a lesser degree, appointment of governors and direct pressure on them are further avenues of political influence that have been employed, at least on occasion.

The authors of the US Banking Act of 1935, which established the FOMC in its modern form, implemented the system of long overlapping terms for governors and shorter renewable terms for the chairman and vice-chairman. It seems to me they made a conscious effort to balance independence and accountability. The short, renewable term for the chairman would enhance accountability and encourage a strong working relationship between the chairman and the executive and legislative branches. On the other hand, the long and effectively non-renewable terms for governors would protect the fundamental independence of monetary policy. So the Federal Reserve Bank loses points in some indices of independence because of the short term of the chairman, but the resulting balance between independence and accountability has, in my view, contributed over the years to a successful relationship between the central bank and the rest of government.

It appears to me that with the current decentralization of the administration in the Congo, there is room for a strong legislative agenda to revise the structure and functioning of the Central Bank of the Congo in such a way as to strengthen its independence and accountability. The Federal Reserve System provides a clear model to be emulated in this respect.

Transparency as a tool for greater accountability

Transparency and disclosure are also essential to accountability. Transparency refers to being easily understood. With respect to monetary policy, it refers to the immediacy with which the public learns of policy decisions and the amount of information provided about the rationale for policy actions and the assessment of how possible future developments bear on policy. The legislature, for example, needs information about the policy actions and an understanding of the rationale for the policy if it is to be able to hold the central bank accountable. In addition, it is generally agreed that markets work better with more complete information, although some worry that a continuous flow of information on the leanings of members of the policy committee can result in excessive volatility in financial markets.

Over time the Parliament has to make efforts to increase the transparency of the monetary policy process and widen the scope of disclosures of monetary policy decisions and of the discussions leading up to those decisions. Historically, the Central Bank of the Congo has responded initially by trying to preserve the status quo. Hopefully, over time, it will come to accept and even appreciate the evolution towards greater transparency and disclosure. Continuing concerns would be the potentially deleterious effect of still greater transparency and disclosure on the effectiveness of the deliberative process and the possible effects on the volatility of financial markets.

Transparency is influenced by the operating procedures used to implement monetary policy. It is furthered by announcements of policy changes, along with statements explaining the rationale underlying policy actions, and by timely and sufficiently detailed reporting of the substantive discussions leading to the policy decisions.

The Central Bank of the Congo has to begin setting its policy in terms of the tightness of reserve positions (so-called 'reserve market conditions'). However, this could be a very imprecise way of setting and explaining policy, making it more difficult for the public and the Parliament to monitor and evaluate monetary policy decisions. One of the developments of practice under a new governorship should be to set policy explicitly in terms of a target rate for the central bank funds rate.

Initially, these decisions might not be directly conveyed to the public. Instead, the Central Bank of the Congo could alter the way in which it implements open market operations to alert financial markets to the change in policy. In the near future, the Central Bank of the Congo could begin announcing on the day of each meeting any change in its central bank funds target. At the same time, it could begin to offer a brief statement explaining the rationale for the policy change. A policy of issuing a statement even when there is no change in policy will need to be implemented sooner rather than later.

The effect of monetary policy derives not only from the explicit policy actions taken, but also from expectations about future policy. Until quite recently, the Central Bank of the Congo opposed earlier release of its directive or minutes precisely because that would provide some hints about prospects for future policy and this could result in volatility in financial markets. Today, however, not only should the central bank immediately announce its policy decisions and provide a rationale for policy changes, it should also reveal whether it believes the risks to achieving its goals are balanced or unbalanced – and, if unbalanced, in what direction. With this change, the markets would focus considerable attention on what the Central Bank of the Congo says about the future.

Transparency would also be enhanced by disclosure – including the announcement of policy actions and of the rationale for policy actions, the release of a summary in the minutes of the central bank's substantive discussion about the economic outlook and the appropriate course of policy, and testimony before the Parliament. The Central Bank of the Congo should start to release minutes of each meeting shortly after the following meeting – in effect, a delay of six or seven weeks. It would be a further step towards enhanced transparency if the release process could be speeded up.

The transcripts of an entire year of meetings – lightly edited verbatim records of the deliberations, with reductions for sensitive information related to foreign governments or specific businesses or individuals – should be released with a lag of five years. The decision to do so could be approved by Parliament with immediate effect. Until now, it is has not been widely known – inside or outside the Central Bank of the Congo – that verbatim records of meetings (transcribed from audio tapes) are retained. Once the minutes are released, the tapes themselves are erased – actually taped over – in conformance with the central bank directives. I presume that once the Parliament has learned of the availability of the transcripts, it will demand that they be released to the public, and the procedures for doing so will be negotiated between the Central Bank of the Congo and the Parliament. The transcripts would be a useful historical record of the central bank meetings and provide scholars as well as board members with insights into the monetary policy process and its evolution over time.

Central Bank of the Congo versus the executive branch

Independence and accountability – important as these concepts are – do not effectively convey the full richness of the relationship of the Central

Bank of the Congo to the rest of the government. The relationship in practice is, after all, as much informal as formal. Informal relationships, and even the effectiveness of formal ones, also have a lot to do with personalities as well as with institutional history and traditions. And these informal relationships are, in turn, important channels for political influence.

One important reason for consultation and communication between the Central Bank of the Congo and both the executive and legislative branches is the desirability of effective coordination of monetary and fiscal policies. The executive and legislative branches collectively set fiscal policy, while the central bank sets monetary policy. The appropriate monetary policy must give substantial weight to prevailing and expected fiscal policies. To a lesser degree, the same principle is at work in the formation of fiscal policies. I say to a lesser extent because, in my opinion, fiscal policies since the early 1970s have been set more on the basis of short-run considerations – such as meeting the conditionalities under the ill-conceived stabilization programmes rather than promoting long-term economic growth. As a result, stabilization policy has always been principally the main concern of the central bank and the fiscal authorities except under extreme circumstances. The forecast of the central bank must consider current and prospective fiscal policies, and monetary policy must adjust to fiscal policy changes, while the executive and legislative branches are somewhat freer to implement changes in long-run strategies as the political consensus allows or dictates.

Figure 2.8 The Presidency of the Democratic Republic of the Congo in Kinshasa

On the other hand, the absence of active stabilization efforts by the executive branch (and the Parliament) might increase their frustration about the stabilization policies pursued by the Central Bank of the Congo – or perhaps more likely at the perceived failure of the Central Bank of the Congo to pursue full employment aggressively enough – and increase efforts at political interference with the conduct of monetary policy.

The relationship between the Central Bank of the Congo and the executive branch has evolved over the last fifty years towards a more informal and less structured relationship. The 1 + 3 transitional administration (one president and three vice-presidents) established an Advisory Committee on Economic and Financial Matters (EcoFin) which included the governor of the Central Bank of the Congo, the president's economic and financial adviser, the key economic ministers (including the finance minister, the budget minister, and the minister of state portfolio) – plus other relevant sectoral ministers. With the minister of finance in the lead, the EcoFin functioned as a forum for frequent consultations on the policy mix. During that period, fiscal policy had a more prominent role in stabilization policy, with monetary policy playing a more supporting and accommodating role. The central bank governor has also acted as a close adviser to the president of the Republic in discussions unrelated to the coordination of stabilization policy.

The current elected Congolese administration inherited the recession and budget deficits of the 1 + 3 model and is clearly determined to use fiscal policy to promote stabilization and recovery. In the prelude to the September 2007 US$8.5 billion Chinese credit to the Democratic Republic of the Congo, the Central Bank Governor was included in policy discussions as part of 'the Congolese Financial Team' consisting also of the minister of finance, the minister of budget, the minister of infrastructures and the presidential economic and financial adviser. The Governor was included mainly to ensure that the Central Bank of the Congo acted in its capacity as the economic and financial adviser to the government on such issues and to ensure that the effect of such a large infusion of foreign capital was fully assessed and taken into account for monetary policy consideration.

Today, the interaction between the Central Bank of the Congo and the administration is more informal but also perhaps more continuous. However, that relationship is less focused on monetary–fiscal policy coordination than on regulatory and international economic issues as well as on cash management and budget execution issues. This situation reflects the smaller role of monetary policy and fiscal policy in longer-run issues related to encouraging more rapid trend growth. It reflects the focus on stabilization policies imposed through an economic agenda designed with assistance from Bretton Woods institutions.

The minister of finance and the governor of the Central Bank of the Congo should meet frequently, for breakfast or lunch, at least once a week. The meetings should be generally short (but need not be always), with no formal agenda and no staff. These meetings ought to be complementary to regular telephone consultations and should become the main source of ongoing contact between the governor and the administration.

There ought to be a number of other opportunities for regular contact between the Central Bank of the Congo and members of the administration's economic team. A central bank board member (on a rotating basis) should host a weekly lunch for senior staff of the Ministry of Finance and the Central Bank of the Congo. While the meetings would often be social as well as substantive, there would be opportunities to discuss issues of mutual concern. Some of the most effective meetings would be 'theme' meetings, when participants agree in advance to focus on a particular issue. Given the stated Ministry of Finance's respect for the independence of the Central Bank, participants would rarely discuss monetary policy, although they would occasionally touch on the economic outlook. Regulatory issues, debt management or international economic issues would tend to dominate. But the contacts made and refreshed at these meetings could be extremely constructive when discussions between the Central Bank of the Congo and the Ministry of Finance or the government are called for, again most often on regulatory issues.

Members of the board of the Central Bank of the Congo and members of the president's Economic and Financial Advisory Office also need to meet monthly for lunch. Once again, discussions of the economic outlook and monetary policy would be rare. But the discussions could often involve interesting issues related to the economic outlook, such as the sources of the increases in productivity growth and why most other countries have or have not benefited significantly thus far from the same developments.

The president and the governor of the Central Bank of the Congo would need to meet occasionally – generally at least four times a year. These meetings would typically be informal discussions without agendas and without announcements before or after the meetings. They would also include the prime minister, the minister of finance, and the president's chief of staff. These would typically be opportunities for the governor to brief the president on the Congolese and global economic outlooks. The frequency of meetings between the governor and both the minister of finance and the president would vary, depending to an important degree on the individuals involved.

The Central Bank of the Congo and the Ministry of Finance would participate in a variety of working groups – including the President's Working Group on Financial Markets and Economic Development. The Ministry of Finance and the Central Bank of the Congo officials often serve together on Congolese delegations to international organizations including: meetings of Bretton Woods institutions, finance ministers and central bank governors; regional organizations such as the African Development Bank, the CEAC and SADC Discussions Groups, and the Forum for African Central Bank Governors; the Financial Stability Forum, and G-24; and bilateral economic dialogues, for example, with China, South Africa, Zambia, Angola, the European Union, the United States, and so on. Before each such forum, it is typical for the Congolese delegation to meet together to coordinate their participation and views.

Central Bank of the Congo versus Parliament

The Central Bank of the Congo's independence is a product of parliamentary legislation and can therefore be diminished at the will of the Parliament unless the president of the Republic exercises his privilege of veto. The Parliament should have such authority if its oversight of the Central Bank of the Congo is to be credible and effective. This power is a rather blunt instrument, providing ample opportunity for the Central Bank of the Congo to take advantage of its independence in the conduct of monetary policy. At the same time, it ensures that the Central Bank of the Congo is extremely respectful of the oversight authority of the Parliament and provides some leverage for parliamentary influence on the conduct of monetary policy. In assessing parliamentary influence, it is also useful to distinguish between the views of a vocal minority and the consensus view – insofar as it can be ascertained – of the Parliament.

It is sometimes difficult to separate direct political involvement in monetary policy from essential parliamentary oversight of monetary policy. In the current situation, it might be considered inappropriate for the administration to comment directly on the conduct of monetary policy, though this may reflect the extraordinary relationship between this administration and the Central Bank of the Congo and the exceptional economic environment of the last several years. Only time will tell. At any rate, for the time being, the relationship between the administration and the Central Bank of the Congo on monetary policy should be

Figure 2.9 The Parliament building in Kinshasa

confined to presidential appointments to the board while the members of the administration and the board (and especially the governor and the Ministry of Finance) engage in regular but informal consultations. On the other hand, the Parliament cannot fulfil its oversight responsibilities without actively engaging the Central Bank of the Congo in a dialogue about the conduct of monetary policy.

The Parliament could convey its views on monetary policy through a variety of vehicles, including letters, speeches, statements and questions at hearings, committee reports on monetary policy, and bills and resolutions. The Parliament over the years would have to use a variety of approaches to influence monetary policy. Perhaps most important, Parliament needs to set the goals for monetary policy in law. In addition, the Senate would need to confirm nominees to the Board of Directors of the central bank, although there is a danger that individual senators might hold up board member confirmations in an attempt to influence policy and appointments. The Parliament could, if it decided, pass legislation that directly requires a specific monetary policy action. The Parliament could threaten to change the structure of the Central Bank of the Congo – to abolish the Central Bank of the Congo at the extreme, or specify particular qualifications for board members, or alter the composition of the Board of Directors – in an attempt to influence monetary policy. The Parliament could demand an accounting of policy by summoning the governor and board members to parliamentary hearings, in addition to the formal semi-annual testimonies by the governor.

The line between oversight and direct involvement in the conduct of policy might certainly be crossed if the Parliament passed or even introduced a resolution or legislation that gave a specific direction to raise or lower interest rates and, especially, when such a direction is accompanied by proposed legislation that would reduce the independence of the Central Bank of the Congo. Such a situation is to be avoided at all costs for the sake of policy credibility.

The recent history since the beginning of the third Republic shows that members of the Parliament do try to influence monetary policy, especially when the economy is performing poorly or when interest rates are high or rising, but Parliament has rarely gone so far as to pass legislation to direct policy. In fact, if such legislation is introduced, it is rarely passed. But simply proposing the introduction of such legislative mandates might be one way in which the Parliament tries to persuade the Central Bank of the Congo to alter its conduct of monetary policy.

At the most extreme end of efforts to change the structure of the Central Bank of the Congo, bills could be introduced to repeal the Central Bank of the Congo Act (thereby abolishing the central bank altogether), to remove board members, or even to impeach the governor of the Central Bank of the Congo and all the members of the Board of Directors at the same time. This eventuality is certainly possible in a democracy, but it should never be allowed to succeed for the sake of the credibility of the central bank.

In return for granting the Central Bank of the Congo 'independence', the Parliament asks three things. First, the central bank must do a good job promoting the objectives that the Parliament has identified. Second, it must accept a certain amount of grumbling about the decisions that impose short-run costs, especially when unemployment is high or policy tightens pre-emptively to contain what the Central Bank of the Congo perceives as inflation risks. The Central Bank of the Congo is always the one taking away the punch bowl just as the party is getting good, with members of the Parliament among those who always question the timing of any restraint. To be fair, members of the Parliament would be among the first to congratulate the Central Bank of the Congo when rates are lowered! And there will always be plenty of praise for the Central Bank of the Congo's contribution to the country's exceptional economic performance when things go right. Third, the Central Bank of the Congo must be fully prepared to accept a substantial part of the blame for bad results (whether or not it caused them).

In return, Parliament ought to keep its part of the bargain by leaving the core of central bank operations alone, so long as things go right, and intervening only around the edges (hearings, speeches, letters, and the introduction of an occasional bill or resolution) to show that it remains alert to its oversight responsibilities and to reflect the concerns of the public.

The appointment process is an important element of the relationship with the Parliament. The governor and the members of the Board of Directors have to be subject to confirmation by the Senate. As we have seen, the confirmation process is sometimes a way for the Parliament to influence the conduct of the BCC's policy, just as the appointment process offers this opportunity to the president. When the president and the parliamentary majority are from different parties, party politics can affect the Central Bank of the Congo and may explain, in part, why today the board has a governor who is serving after the expiration of his term (since a governor can continue to serve in such a case until reappointed or until a new governor is appointed and confirmed). Delayed action on nominations for board members, or reappointment as governor, can serve as a vehicle for some senators to express displeasure with the conduct of monetary policy.

Another important relationship with the Parliament is through hearings. The governor of the Central Bank of the Congo has to testify frequently before the Parliament (with a mandatory limit of twenty-five hearings per year at the maximum under exceptional circumstances), with most of the hearings being about monetary policy. Other members of the Board of Directors may testify also, though less frequently, with a range of eight to twenty-two appearances per year. Typically the governor alone would testify on monetary policy. The most important testimony on monetary policy is delivered at semi-annual hearings before the Parliament and the Senate. But the governor is not invited for many other hearings, including appearances before the budget committees, the Joint Economic Committee of the National Assembly and the Senate, and the banking committees.

In addition, on rare occasions, the governor and other board members meet with members of the National Assembly and the Senate, either at the Central Bank of the Congo or the Parliament, mostly at the request of the legislators. These meetings are rarely about monetary policy and mostly focus on regulatory issues, including banking bills and community reinvestment issues, but they are also sometimes about global economic developments, international financial crises, or international financial architecture issues. In addition, contact at the staff level between the Board of Directors of the Central Bank of the Congo and parliamentary committees is expected to become common. The bank's staff will routinely be asked for technical assistance in drafting legislation on banking, consumer protection, and amendments to the existing legislation and other areas.

Finally, members of the Parliament often write letters to the Board of Directors of the Central Bank of the Congo – individually and in groups – typically urging a specific direction for monetary policy. Most of these letters are opportunities to express concern about high interest rates or, in most cases, to urge the directors either to not raise interest rates or to lower them.

These letters should perhaps be best understood as attempts by the Parliament to alert the Central Bank of the Congo to the painful effects on constituents as a by-product of the conduct of monetary policy – typically when the Central Bank of the Congo pre-emptively raises interest rates in an effort to prevent higher inflation or tries to unwind an earlier increase in inflation, or when it is not stimulating a sluggish economy sufficiently. Having admonished the Central Bank of the Congo in an effort to make sure it understands the consequences of its policies, the Parliament generally relies on the Central Bank of the Congo to balance inflation and stabilization objectives, which is the implicit contract of the regime in which the Parliament has delegated instrument independence to the Central Bank of the Congo.

Independence and accountability: unresolved issues

In my opinion, the Central Bank of the Congo statutes – together with the policy-making structure as amended by Law no. 005/2002, the policy mandate introduced in 2002, and the informal relationships that have evolved – have resulted on paper in an excellent trade-off between independence and accountability for the Central Bank of the Congo. Nevertheless, the resulting equilibrium still offers opportunities for political influence; therefore sustaining central bank independence will require that independence is built into a lasting tradition within the Central Bank of the Congo and that will depend on the strength of will and public prestige of the governor, in particular, and also of other central bank board members, in resisting efforts at political control. However, controversies linger about whether or not the policy mandate should be refined and whether transparency and disclosure should be further enhanced now that an elected National Assembly and an elected Senate are in place.

The legislative mandate under which the Central Bank of the Congo operates is different from the mandate applied to most other central banks. It explicitly sets out a single mandate for monetary policy in addition to other functions that the central bank is asked to accomplish. Should there be short-run conflicts between these functions and the price stability objective, the statutes do not identify any priority between the multiple objectives. There is a small group in the Parliament who would like to revise the language related to the policy mandate to elevate the role of price stability to the single monetary policy among the different central bank actions. They press this issue not only out of dissatisfaction with the conduct of monetary policy but because they believe such a revised policy mandate would strengthen the credibility of the Central Bank of the Congo's commitment to price stability and thereby allow the central bank to carry out this commitment in the most efficient way. However, a larger group in the Parliament has mixed views on the BCC's commitment to promoting other economic objectives such as full employment through its conduct of monetary policy.

A related issue is the precision with which the objectives should be stated. The mandate, for example, sets out other objectives – including supervision of the financial sector and cashier to the government, full employment through a strong support to the government economic programme, and price stability – but leaves it up to the Central Bank of the Congo to define these goals precisely. As recent experience confirms, it would be difficult and unwise to set any numerical target for full employment, given the uncertainty about what that target should be, and the likelihood that this target would vary over time with demographic changes in the labour force, government policies, and changes in the efficiency of the matching process between jobs and unemployed workers. The Central Bank of the Congo has never set an explicit numerical target for inflation. I would like to suggest that we define price stability as inflation so low and stable that it no longer affects the decisions of households and businesses. However, today, a growing number of governments have set explicit numerical targets for their central banks at no more than 2 per cent on an annual basis. Based on this knowledge and considering the buoyancy of the Congolese economy and its current dependence on imported goods (from countries with an annual inflation target of 2 per cent), I would like to suggest that the Central Bank of the Congo aim at an annual inflation rate of no more than 4 per cent.

A second broad issue has to do with transparency and disclosure. Over the years, there has been an evolution towards greater disclosure and transparency. Financial and organizational audits of the Central Bank of the Congo have revealed important weaknesses which need to be addressed urgently. I believe, therefore, that we ought to be looking for opportunities for further progress. The major questions relate to the release of the minutes and of the transcripts following meetings of the central bank board. Introducing this as a tradition would significantly improve the standing and credibility of the Central Bank of the Congo.

Conclusion

In an emerging democracy, it is important to balance the independence of a central bank with some degree of accountability. But as we have seen, these concepts do not always capture the complexity of the relationship between the central bank and government. The relationship in practice is both informal and formal. The effectiveness of formal or informal relationships depends on personalities as well as institutional history and traditions, and informal relationships are of course important channels for political influence.

To reiterate what has been said above, the president of a country and the governor of the central bank need to meet occasionally – generally at least four times a year. These meetings should typically be informal discussions without agendas and without announcements before or after the meetings. They would also include the prime minister, the minister of finance, and the president's chief of staff. The meetings are an opportunity for the governor to brief the president on the national and global economic outlooks. The frequency of meetings between the governor and the minister of finance should be on a weekly basis to ensure good communication on important issues.

Parliament can convey its views on monetary policy through a variety of vehicles, including letters, speeches, statements and questions at hearings, committee reports on monetary policy, and bills and resolutions. The line between oversight and direct involvement in the conduct of policy might well be crossed if the Parliament passes or even introduces a resolution or legislation that gives specific direction to raise or lower interest rates and, especially, when such directions are accompanied by proposed legislation that would reduce the independence of the central bank. The Parliament ought to leave the core of central bank operations alone, so long as things go smoothly, and intervene only around the edges (through hearings, speeches, letters and the introduction of an occasional bill or resolution) in order to show that they are alert to their oversight responsibilities and reflect the concerns of their constituents.

The appointment process is an important element of the relationship with the Parliament. The governor and Board of Directors' members have to be subject to confirmation by the Senate. The confirmation process would be a way for the Parliament to influence the conduct of central bank policy, just as the appointment and reappointment process offers this opportunity to the president.

While the relationship between the central bank and the executive or legislative branches of government is very important, it is critical to look at the way monetary policy is or ought to be conducted behind closed doors. This analysis leads us to propose a new monetary policy agenda to move from the failed 'business-as-usual' practices into a new professional setting conducive to effective policy design and implementation in an emerging economy.

3
A Practical Perspective on the New Monetary Policy Agenda

In this chapter, I intend to discuss a proposal on the making of a new kind of monetary policy, providing a glimpse into what might go on behind closed doors in Kinshasa. Then, I will describe some of the challenges faced by monetary policy-makers, as well as how the Central Bank of the Congo might evolve to handle these issues.

The chapter is intended to provide a better understanding of the many complexities and uncertainties surrounding the Congolese economy and its financial system, as well as the evolving role that monetary policy must play in their progress. It is to be hoped that Congolese policy-makers and the public will share my view that the Central Bank of the Congo and the proposed MPC or NOMC could prove to be very effective mechanisms for making sound monetary policy decisions.

Setting the new monetary policy agenda

The Central Bank of the Congo is an enigma to many people. If you ask most people what the Central Bank of the Congo does, they might say that it stores cash, that it sets the interest rate and that this has a big impact on the economy. If you ask who in the Central Bank makes this decision, or how they decide, most people will say that the governor of the BCC does so. But in reality, it is actually or should be a committee decision. Having discussed the structure and functions of central banks in general we now focus upon the role that the proposed Monetary Policy Committee or National Open Market Committee could play in directing monetary policy in the Democratic Republic of the Congo.

The Central Bank of the Congo is the epicentre of the financial system. It controls the money supply of the economy, ensures the integrity of the financial system, and provides liquidity in times of crisis. The Central

Bank's mission is to provide money and credit conditions in the form of price stability that fosters maximum economic growth and full employment on a sustained basis. Whether the Central Bank actually does what it is supposed to do is a different matter.

The proposed monetary policy

The central bank's control of money and credit conditions in the economy is the core of what is referred to as monetary policy. This process of injecting or withdrawing liquidity in the financial markets accelerates or retards output growth and alters inflation pressures in the economy.

The Law on the Central Bank of the Congo clearly lays out the goals of monetary policy. It explicitly states that in conducting monetary policy the Central Bank should seek to promote stable prices, moderate long-term interest rates and pursue maximum employment.

Monetary policy is a dynamic process, set with due consideration for the current conditions in the national economy. To achieve its goals, the central bank must ascertain where the economy is, where it is headed, and whether that direction is appropriate. If not, the central bank must take action to attempt to move the economy in a direction that is more consistent with its long-run objectives. This process requires constant vigilance and continual interaction with the markets to maintain financial conditions that are appropriate for maximum sustainable growth and price stability.

Advisable tools of monetary policy

The Central Bank of the Congo has three principal instruments at its disposal – direct open market operations, the *taux directeur* or discount rate, and reserve requirements – that can be used in support of these objectives.

Open market operations refer to the purchase or sale of government securities or purchase or sale of foreign currencies against the Congolese franc by the Central Bank, with the effect of injecting liquidity into or withdrawing it from the financial markets. Decisions about open market operations are to be made by a specific committee within the central bank, the proposed Monetary Policy Committee (MPC) or the National Open Market Committee (NOMC).

The *taux directeur* or *discount rate* is the interest rate charged to banking institutions when they borrow from the central bank. This rate would be set by the National Open Market Committee or the Monetary Policy Committee.

Reserve requirements are the amount of funds that a banking institution must hold in the central bank against its deposit liabilities. Banking institutions in the DRC must hold these reserves in the form of vault cash or deposits with the Central Bank of the Congo. Within limits specified by law, the National Open Market Committee, or the MPC, could unilaterally change reserve requirements, increasing or decreasing the banking sector's ability to provide credit to the economy.

In practice, changes in the *taux directeur* or discount rate, for the most part, would be made to keep the *taux directeur* or discount rate in appropriate relation to other short-term interest rates. Therefore, *taux directeur* or discount rate changes can be thought of as complementary to open market operations. By contrast, changes in reserve requirements would be rare, and would not be used in the routine conduct of monetary policy. So, open market operations would be the principal instrument of monetary policy – which would make the MPC or NOMC the principal decision-making body with respect to national monetary policy.

Yet, the drafters of the Central Bank of the Congo Law of 2002 did not establish the MPC or the NOMC, nor did they have any idea of their potential future importance at the time. So, where does the idea of the MPC or NOMC come from? And, how can it be established in practice?

Implementing the new monetary policy agenda

As I noted at the outset, the Central Bank of the Congo was established with the passage of the Central Bank of the Congo Law of 2002. By design, the Central Bank does receive an appropriation from Parliament. But because it is viewed as a bankers' bank, it has to move progressively to fund itself from the return on its assets and from fees for its services to commercial banks. It is the Central Bank's self-funding mechanism that has now planted the seeds of change that ultimately can lead to the emergence of the MPC or NOMC as the primary monetary policy-making body.

It is with the intention of funding its own operations that the Central Bank of the Congo would have to begin purchasing debt securities in the local market. Gradually, it has been recognized that the Central Bank's open market securities transactions (although occasional and limited) have a powerful and immediate impact on short-term interest rates and the supply of money and credit. Over time, open market operations should become the central tool for carrying out monetary policy, replacing the discount window and periodic changes in required reserves.

So how is it possible for all of this to happen? How would the National Open Market Committee or Monetary Policy Committee go about setting its reserve funds rate target?

The mechanics of the new monetary policy agenda

The MPC or NOMC would have eight scheduled meetings per year. These meetings would usually be sufficient to conduct MPC or NOMC business. However, when circumstances dictate, the MPC or NOMC could convene quickly to address a situation requiring immediate attention.

During scheduled MPC or NOMC meetings, a standard agenda would be followed. The meetings would include a combination of both presentations and discussion, covering developments in both the domestic and international markets, the state of the Congolese economy, and the potential need for policy adjustment.

Perhaps most important for the meetings and adding immense value to the process would be the diverse professional experience of the participants. With backgrounds ranging from banking, finance and economic forecasting to academia, each participant would bring his or her own perspective to the issues. Although the forecasts are based on sophisticated econometric modelling, it is the collective judgement of this group of individuals that would bring the NOMC or MPC to a policy decision. This decision would be announced to the markets at the end of the meeting.

Most meetings would be one-day events, running from 9.00 a.m. to about 1.00 p.m. Although perhaps meeting only twice a year, the MPC or NOMC members would meet for two days to broaden their discussion beyond the immediate policy decision and examine specific topics. The policy portion of every meeting would begin with a review of recent events in both financial and foreign exchange markets, and a review of the details of open market operations since the last meeting. The Central Bank's manager of the Open Market Operations would lead this discussion.

Next, the director of research and statistics at the Central Bank of the Congo would present a report on the state of the national economy and the staff's forecast of where the economy is heading. He or she would include considerable detail on both the current state of the national economy, and prospects for the future using a large-scale econometric model. This would then be supplemented by an overview of the international situation by the head of the international division at the Central

Bank. A thorough exchange of views, with questions and answers, debate and discussions, would all be part of the process of sharing views and increasing understanding.

There would be a lot of material to analyse and understand. The forecast would be assembled into a book with a green cover referred to as the Green Book. After the presentation of the staff forecast, the debate will become more lively. With the exception of the governor, each member – that is, twelve NOMC or MPC members plus specialized directors of the Central Bank – will present his or her views on the national and international economy.

The MPC or NOMC members from the provinces generally would provide in-depth and real-time information regarding developments in their own communities. They would also focus on industries that have a high concentration in their local market area. For example, one would expect the review of regional conditions in the Katanga or Kasai provinces to lend insight into the mining sector; Bas-Congo covers a region that is heavily dependent on electricity generation, and so on. As Kinshasa has become much more diverse and quite representative of the entire national economy, its perspective would therefore tend to mirror what is happening over all of these sectors.

This discussion would provide valuable 'tone and feel' information about economic activity throughout the country. To this end, the Central Bank will have to spend a good deal of time collecting up-to-date intelligence on current and likely future economic conditions from different sectors of the economy and informal 'town meetings' around the country.

Next the committee members would move to the most crucial stage of the meeting: the discussion of policy options and a policy action plan. To focus the discussion, the director of the Division of Monetary Affairs, who would be secretary to the Committee, would outline the options before the NOMC or MPC members. This is no small challenge. He is not supposed to second guess the Committee or to make a recommendation for a particular policy action, but rather to present a clear and objective case for the range of actions the Committee may wish to consider, offering both the pros and cons surrounding the policy under consideration. Typically, three options would be considered, most often centring on (a) should interest rates be moved up, (b) down, or (c) kept the same? This analysis too is sent to the MPC or NOMC participants in advance in a second book to be known as the Blue Book for its blue cover.

Having heard all the arguments and data and weighing people's views, the governor would then offer his own perspective on where the economy is, what the risks are, and what appears to be the appropriate policy going forward.

This is followed by a second round of discussion in which all of the participants react to both the policy options presented and the governor's proposal. This process would be lively, as the Committee tries to converge on a consensus. It is likely that some differences of opinion will remain; yet the decision would most often be one that all can support.

This would then be followed by the formal vote. This would be the first time that the twenty or so participants are treated differently, since not all of them would be voting members of the Committee. All twelve NOMC or MPC members, including the seven Central Bank board members would be entitled to vote. Although voting is an important part of the process, up until the vote, all members of the group would have been fully engaged in the discussion, and all members of the MPC or NOMC participate on equal terms, whether or not they are voting at any particular meeting. Consequently, each of the twenty members would play an important part in the consensus building that leads to the formal policy vote.

There are two more important steps in the process. The NOMC or MPC members have decided what to do, but now they must direct the operating parts of the Central Bank to take action consistent with the policy decision, and they must inform the public of the actions.

The first procedure is reasonably straightforward. The Central Bank Open Market Desk will be instructed to alter its pattern of purchases and sales in the financial market so as to cause the Central Bank *taux directeur* to move to the new target or to maintain the target if no change is being made.

Next, the MPC or NOMC will consider its public announcement. When the Committee votes on the policy action, the press release would be discussed at some length. The goal here would be to inform the market not only what committee members have decided but why.

Transition to a strong central bank

As many readers may know, Jean Claude Masangu's second and last five-year term at the Central Bank came to an end in August 2007. Much has been written about this, but little has been written explaining *why* there had to be a transition at all.

Members of the Board of Directors of the Central Bank of the Congo are nominated by the president and have to be confirmed by the Senate according to the Constitution of the Democratic Republic of the Congo.

A governor's full term of office is ten years, and the selected individual may sit for only two full and successive terms of five years each. This was the case for Governor Jean Claude Masangu. He was appointed in August 1997 for a five-year term that ended in August 2002 which was renewed for another and last five-year term ending in August 2007. At that time, the president of the Republic selected and appointed the nominee, but there was no Senate confirmation. With the new Constitution in effect since February 2006, there is a need for the Central Bank of the Congo to effect a clear transition into the future. Nominated candidates for the governorship and to the Board of Directors or the NOMC or MPC would have to meet a number of qualifications, including passage before the Senate for their confirmation.

It is worth noting that Jean Claude Masangu is the first governor of the Central Bank of the Congo to serve two consecutive full terms totalling ten years. This has set a good precedent in the history of the Central Bank of the Congo where the turnover of governors has been among the highest in the world.

Now, as the Masangu era has come to an end, the country must look ahead to the challenges it will face under a new governor in an increasingly complex economic environment. The new leader of the Central Bank of the Congo may have his or her own way of doing things; some aspects of the process of policy-making may change as a new governor directs both the Board of Directors and the MPC or NOMC.

Under new leadership, processes and policies are often reviewed and restructured. This can mean simple things: for example, perhaps a move towards electronic dissemination of documents; or more substantive things, such as a move to inflation targeting, which some MPC or NOMC members might be willing to support. Nonetheless, I am confident that the passing of the torch from Governor Masangu to his successor will be smooth and seamless. For one thing, while processes may change, the Central Bank's mission will not. The mandate of fostering a stable price environment will remain firmly in place and will receive a new impetus as new leadership brings new ideas.

Our nation's Central Bank consists of more than one person. In addition to the governor, the policy process also requires or will require the input of the other six members of the Board of Directors or the proposed twelve MPC or NOMC members. All would attend MPC or NOMC meetings, participate in the discussions, and contribute to the Committee's assessment of the economy and policy options. The result would be a dynamic mix of keen insight and intellect, of economic analysis and interpretation, and of stewardship and policy-making from some of the best economic minds in the nation.

Having been governor for ten years, Jean Claude Masangu has unquestionably left his mark on the Central Bank. Having had the pleasure of following the activities of the Central Bank very closely over the last ten years, I believe that Governor Masangu's successor has much to do if the Bank is to live up to the challenges and policy changes underlined in this book. However, despite the challenges posed by any transition, I have no doubt that the Central Bank of the Congo will continue to grow and evolve under its new leadership.

Media reports endlessly dissect the upcoming transition of leadership at the Central Bank of the Congo. They cite widespread concern over large fiscal budget and international trade deficits, as well as concerns over potentially growing inflationary pressures, the state of the financial system and ever-present political uncertainties. They lament the passing of the baton from Masangu, who, during his governorship, saw the exchange rates plummet from 1.3 francs to the dollar in 1998 to as much as 565 francs to the dollar in March 2008.

Of course, the Masangu era was special, particularly because the Central Bank's business had to face the issues arising from financing the war and protecting and defending national sovereignty. Governor Masangu served for over ten years under two presidents of the Republic, and during his tenure, the Congolese economy had trouble achieving both strong growth and stable prices. On average, from 1997 to 2007, the annual inflation rate was 139 per cent, which is mainly attributed to the consequences and demands of war in an environment where it was not possible to ascertain the independence of the monetary authority. Inside the Central Bank, Governor Masangu, like his predecessor Djamboleka Loma, exhibited a powerful influence and fundamentally altered the way Central Bank staff think about policy-making and public service.

It was perhaps difficult to accomplish much while the country was at war with Rwanda, Uganda and Burundi. Masangu did his best during a tough time and cannot be blamed for the economic troubles of the country during his tenure. It is not obvious that a different governor with different approaches and skills could have done any better during the last ten years. As a banker, the outgoing governor has shown a most remarkable ability to adapt to the changes in the political environment and he has listened carefully to the government's needs during the times of war.

But if Masangu's successor needs to be an extraordinary banker, he will also have to be an extraordinary leader in order to succeed in turning the Central Bank around. He will have to be a consensus builder and a developer of talent. This would be measured in the strength of the organization and the strong consensus that would have to be achieved at monetary policy meetings. Unanimity would be the rule, not the exception, in spite of strong voices and difficult circumstances. If this is achieved it will be a testament to the new leadership and the basis for a strong Central Bank for years to come.

Transparency

Historians will probably remember the next governor of the Central Bank of the Congo for the changes that are made to the transparency of Central Bank policy-making over the next decade. This openness will be the defining aspect of the future monetary policy under a new governor. The future governor of the Central Bank of the Congo will have to put communication on Central Bank activities at the heart of his or her action and tenure. He or she must communicate publicly more often than any other governor has done in the history of the Central Bank of the Congo.

For the future, the proposed MPC or NOMC will have to strive for greater transparency, and its communication with the markets will need to improve over the next decade. Information about the Central Bank's policy goals, its assessment of the current economic situation, and its strategic direction will need to become increasingly part of the public record.

The goal of all these steps would be to inform markets about where the MPC or NOMC sees the economy today and where it thinks the economy is headed in the future. This should prove to be useful information that would improve the markets' understanding of the Central Bank's view of the economy and offer them insights into the direction of possible future policy actions.

It is important for the MPC or NOMC to be as open as possible. My hope is that if the central bank provides relevant information, its actions will be more transparent and surprises will become the exception rather than the rule. The record shows that efforts towards transparency have been steps in the right direction. Although monetary policy over the past ten years has not significantly reduced the economic volatility as the Central Bank has not been able to maintain a strong commitment to a stable price environment, notwithstanding the recent recession caused by the war the Congolese economy has the potential to perform quite well over the next decade or so. The restructuring and strengthening of the Central Bank of the Congo will enable it to play a leading role in the process of the reconstruction of the economy.

Challenges to monetary policy

Although we can take comfort from the way the Central Bank of the Congo operates, the proposed Committee's task in going forward is not without its share of challenges which could constitute the limits and limitations that the Central Bank might continue to face when conducting real-time monetary policy.

However, before listing these ongoing challenges, they have to be put in context. The Bank's policy since the country's independence has demonstrated both the value of, and the Central Bank's commitment to, a stable price environment. Hyperinflation has been the number one enemy. Another thing we have learned – and it has been an expensive lesson – is that the best the Central Bank of the Congo can do, is to cushion the economy. It cannot in and of itself force stronger growth than the economy is capable of delivering. Trying to push an economy beyond its potential may temporarily accelerate growth, but it also creates imbalances and increases inflationary pressures that must be addressed, and so boom leads to bust. So looking ahead, the Central Bank of the Congo will need to take policy actions consistent with economic fundamentals and keep its focus on long-run objectives.

Nonetheless, every day, successful monetary policy faces plenty of real-world challenges. It requires an evaluation of where the economy is, where it is going, and where it should be going. The appropriate conduct of real-time monetary policy requires policy-makers to gauge how strong or weak the economy is at any moment in time, what its most likely trajectory appears to be, and how that trajectory aligns with its long-run potential.

This requires a detailed appraisal of data and, importantly, of real-time data on the current state of the economy. Unfortunately, these data often give very noisy signals of what is really going on, and the Central Bank's ability to affect the economy is limited by a few very real technical actors. With the above in mind, I close this chapter by listing just a few challenges the Central Bank of the Congo may face under the proposed new arrangement in the conduct of monetary policy.

Uncertain measurement

The first challenge is that the Central Bank has limited capacity to precisely measure and forecast economic conditions in a country as large and complex as the Democratic Republic of the Congo. Lags in data reports, ongoing data revisions, and the imprecision of the large-scale economic models all significantly limit the BCC's ability to use the tools of economic analysis.

In other words, the Central Bank works with data that are released with a lag and are subject to revisions. As research using the Central Bank's real-time data set shows, updates and revisions to data can be substantial enough to change policy-makers' perception of the need for a policy reaction or at least the extent of the policy action. Indeed, the data on which the Central Bank relies in real time can be imprecise enough to distort the tenor of the policy deliberations and the apparent wisdom of alternative policy actions.

Uncertain policy lags

The second challenge in contemplating future policy actions is the long and variable lags associated with the impact of monetary policy actions. It has been estimated that it takes six to eighteen months for monetary actions to fully impact on the economy. Unfortunately, the Central Bank may never know for certain exactly how long the policy lag would be in any given situation, and waiting to find out is not an option. This is why I argue that the MPC or NOMC must focus its efforts on sustaining the expansion and gearing its monetary policy towards long-term growth objectives.

Expectations

A final challenge facing monetary policy relates to the role that expectations play in the Congolese economy. To be sure, the recent past has demonstrated that expectations matter a great deal. As consumers and businesses alter their expectations of the future, their behaviour changes. If their views change dramatically, this can cause a significant change in real demand. In such circumstances, economic activity can change substantially and policy-makers may have to respond.

Most of the time, public expectations move predictably with economic conditions. When jobs are plentiful and incomes are rising, consumer confidence also rises. Conversely, reports of layoffs and declining incomes undermine consumer confidence. Sometimes, though, confidence and expectations about the future shift dramatically for reasons not related to current economic conditions. These shifts can exert an important, independent impact on current spending decisions and, consequently, on the growth in aggregate demand.

The Central Bank of the Congo cannot and should not try to manage public expectations. However, it can help to stabilize them by being as transparent as possible in its own decision-making. It also must recognize that variations in expectations can have real economic effects that may warrant response. To keep abreast of what is going on amongst the public and in the market, the Central Bank of the Congo has constantly to monitor behaviour and assess the economic climate throughout the country through its network of branches nationwide.

Conclusion

This chapter has examined the many complexities and uncertainties surrounding the implementation of monetary policy in the Congolese economy and its financial system. I hope that the reader will share the view that the proposed MPC or NOMC will prove to be an effective mechanism for making sound monetary policy decisions: not necessarily perfect, but effective, and perhaps much better than the current arrangement which has done little to control inflation over the last decade of central banking in the Democratic Republic of the Congo.

4

Building a Credible Central Bank in an Emerging Democracy

The vaults of the Central Bank of the Congo have featured in some colourful news stories that have appeared in local and international newspapers in recent years. First, there is the claim that on the night of 16 May 1997, one of Mobutu's sons made what has been euphemistically described as the 'illicit withdrawal' of $100 million in $100 bills, and an indeterminate amount of gold bullion. If this actually happened (I personally doubt that it did), it was surely quite a job to load this into the tractor-trailer trucks that were said to have carted the money away. A second story reported that the jewels and gold of the colonial era were rescued by one of the previous Central Bank governors which required workers to pump nearly 500,000 gallons of rain water out of the flooded main central bank vault in Kinshasa.

If the Congolese financial system is to develop smoothly, and the Congolese economy is to join the modern industrialized world, the restructured Central Bank of the Congo will have to be much more than a storage facility for currency and priceless objects. Together with the elected government under the third Republic, the Central Bank will have to manage a transition from the old dictatorial style of leadership to a new entity in a democracy, crafting the necessary market-based institutions in the process, and then it will have to set in place a framework capable of delivering stable long-term growth.

Preconditions for a successful central bank

Before getting to the substance of what the new Central Bank of the Congo needs to do and how it will have to go about it, there is an important precondition for success. Every successful financial and economic system is predicated on the idea that investors can keep the fruits of their investments. For this to happen, there has to be credible government action and enforcement of laws to protect property rights.

The ancestors of modern-day Congo were the first to understand this when they created the first unwritten rules governing financial operations. What was true 300 years ago is still true today. With the legal foundations in place in the form of Law no. 005/2002, the Central Bank needs to focus on meeting two principal objectives. First, it must create an environment in which financial institutions can flourish, ensuring stability of the entire system. A banking system that is constantly in crisis or that is not providing necessary financial services to the population is worse than useless. Second, the new Central Bank of the Congo must operate a monetary policy that keeps domestic Congolese inflation under control. Inflation makes doing business in the Democratic Republic of the Congo difficult by increasing risk to both borrowers and lenders, and makes prices unreliable signals. Low inflation is an indispensable foundation for real growth.

To achieve financial stability, the new Central Bank of the Congo needs to encourage the development of a sound banking system based on arm's-length relationships and market incentives. This means chartering banks to prevent unsavoury characters from running them, and setting up a system of supervision that penalizes bad business decisions. Then there are the day-to-day services that the Central Bank would have to provide. These include both the more mundane job of exchanging old, worn currency for new, crisp notes, and the technologically complex task of providing a payments system that allows funds to move among banks and across the country. The establishment or creation of an electronic payments system is essential to the process of intermediation. It would persuade individuals to deposit funds into banks and, in turn, encourage banks to make loans. To ensure that the payments system develops, the government and the Central Bank of the Congo should subsidize the interbank payments system, at least initially, making it cheaper and easier for commercial banks to serve their retail customers.

Success in policy-making is as much an issue of institutional environment as of the people who are put in charge. Over the past several decades, economists have come to a consensus about the best way to design a central bank so that the people who run it can be successful. A central bank must be independent of political pressures, accountable to the public, transparent in its policy actions, and a clear communicator with financial markets and the public. There is also agreement that it is prudent to have policy decisions made by committee rather than by a single individual or the governor alone.

Of these requirements, operational independence is by far the most important. In fact, virtually every high inflation episode in the world, including the Congolese hyperinflation that averaged 139 per cent per year for the period from 1997 to 2007, is a direct consequence of the political subjugation of the central bank. Without alternative sources of revenue, governments turn to the central bank for financing, forcing them to print more and more money. The result, not surprisingly, is high rates of inflation. So the first step in achieving economic stability is to take the printing presses away from the politicians.

As for accountability, transparency and communications, these become crucial once the bank has been made independent. While the manner in which they are implemented depends critically on local culture and so differs across countries, a few things are universal. First, the public announcement of targets for the central bank is the only way to generate credibility. And second, the central bank has to publish key statistics regularly. Many credible central banks publish their balance sheets weekly, and the Central Bank of the Congo would be well advised to do the same thing in the future. But in the end, exactly what they say and how they say it should depend on what works best with the Congolese people or with the people of the country concerned.

All of this is well and good, but what about the transition from the Central Bank of the Congo under the second Republic to the new Central Bank of the Congo starting in the third Republic and beyond? How can the Democratic Republic of the Congo get from where it is today to where it needs to be? Conditions on the ground in the DRC are surely changing by the hour in ways that only people who are there can appreciate. So my recommendations need to be read in that light.

The end of the civil war, the establishment of an independent central bank, the formation of a legal government following the democratic elections in 2006, the establishment of other institutions such as the National Assembly and the Senate following the elections, and the commitment by the elected government to be fiscally responsible, are leading the public to expect that the Democratic Republic of the Congo will experience lower inflation in the near future than during the last decade. There may well be an initial period of high inflation but it will be important that it be brought under control as quickly as possible. Looking at the history, there are two paths that the new Central Bank of the Democratic Republic of the Congo might take to stabilize prices. It could set up a currency board, or it could adopt an inflation target. I favour the inflation targeting approach mainly due to my strong opposition to a currency board because of the loss of freedom it would entail for national monetary policy. The problem with a currency board is twofold. First, since the central bank can no longer print money it cannot operate as a lender to sound banks that come under unjustified attack. The inability to act as a 'lender of last resort' would severely limit the central bank's ability to avert financial crises. Second, a currency board creates the false impression of monetary policy austerity. As the Argentinians learned the hard way, a currency board provides no protection from fiscal excesses. Without fiscal discipline, monetary policy is impotent to control inflation. It does not take much imagination to envisage a national government following in the footsteps of Argentina, and printing its own currency in defiance of the central bank.

Without fiscal discipline, monetary policy is helpless. Looking at the Democratic Republic of the Congo today, we see immediately that this creates a serious risk. Rebuilding the country's physical infrastructure and transforming its economy into a market-based system is going to be very expensive. During the reconstruction phase, the Central Bank is going to be pressured to print money to finance the widening fiscal deficits. It is absolutely essential to find a way to prevent this from happening. My suggestion is that the government should take charge of fiscal policy during the reconstruction, giving the Central Bank some breathing space to confront the inflation problems they will inevitably face. The hope is that the restructured Central Bank of the Congo will be able to control inflation in the short term, thereby building the credibility that is essential to a successful long-term inflation-targeting regime.

What does a central bank do?

The logical next step in developing a definition of efficiency for central banks is to review what activities central banks engage in, or what precisely it is they should do efficiently. Table 4.1 summarizes previous research of these functions as determined in a few cursory reviews of primary central bank activities. Most of the activities listed are recognizable to a casual observer of central banking, with the approaches of the authors varying as to the breadth of the categories described and the detail with which each of them is broken down.

It is interesting to note how varied the summaries are in Table 4.1 regarding central bank functions. Undertaking a more precise analysis of what central banks do, as this chapter is intended to do, requires a review of individual central bank objectives and an analysis of what functions they undertake to meet those objectives.

Table 4.1 What can central banks do?

Study	*Task/roles/functions*
Pollard (2003)	1. Define and implement monetary policy (referred to as the 'primary function' of a central bank) 2. Issue banknotes 3. Conduct foreign exchange operations 4. Hold and manage official reserves 5. Act as the fiscal agent for the government 6. Promote stability of the financial system 7. Supervise and regulate banks (and the related power as a lender of last resort) 8. Implement consumer protection laws 9. Promote the smooth operation of the payments system 10. Collect statistical information 11. Participate in international monetary institutions
White (2001)	1. Issuer of currency 2. Bankers' bank 3. Regulator of commercial banks 4. Lender of last resort 5. Conductor of monetary policy
Fischer (1995)	6. Monetary policy – managing supply of credit and money and determining market interest rates (referred to as the 'essential' central bank function) 7. Determine exchange rate and managing foreign exchange reserves (fully or jointly) 8. Hold reserves of commercial banks 9. Manage the payments system 10. Supervise banks and other financial institutions 11. Lender of last resort 12. Administer deposit insurance 13. Government's banker 14. Administer foreign exchange controls 15. Manage all or part of the national debt 16. Policy research 17. Development banking
Green (2003)	18. Fiscal services to the government 19. Creditors' agent 20. Facilitate settlement of interbank claims 21. Lender of last resort support to banks in crisis

Rethinking what central banks do

Central bank activities

Undertaking a more precise analysis of central bank operational efficiency requires a review of individual central bank legislative objectives and an analysis of what functions they undertake to meet those objectives. This analysis should be as straightforward as reviewing the individual central bank's law and associated legislation, finding its objective and functions and then comparing these to the operational reports and financial data available from the central bank.

Any assessment of whether a central bank is operating efficiently must focus on what existing core operations are conducted or on the activities that are 'central to central banking'. Next, one can move on to the other activities that are ancilliary or supplemental to these existing core functions. Presumably, the justification for granting each of these powers and responsibilities to a central bank is that each of them is necessary to allow it to achieve its objective. If powers or responsibilities are not directly related to the central bank's objective, then there is a strong argument that it should not be burdened with these responsibilities, as carrying them out would only serve to take up management's time and divert the central bank's available resources away from accomplishing its objective.

Central bank existing core functions

The following are seven existing core functions of central banks in the sense that nearly all central banks undertake some or all of these unique central bank activities. This is distinct from an analysis of whether or not central banks *should* in fact undertake all of these activities, a subject to be analysed on a case-by-case basis depending on the circumstances of each central bank and each country.

1. Monetary policy management

As described previously, monetary policy is the primary or essential central bank function given the direct linkage between it and the objective of price and monetary stability instilled in most central bank statutes. Obviously then, the vast majority undertake monetary policy, with about 85 per cent of all central banks conducting independent monetary policy. Those that do not conduct independent monetary policy are members of larger systems such as the Eurosystem of central banks or the CFA zone,[1] or they operate in countries with currency boards, adopt the monetary policy of another central bank, or choose not to exercise granted monetary authority. Although research is noted by Pollard (2003) in the table above as a separate function and it is often listed as a separate function from monetary policy in central bank statutes, the bulk of the research of a central bank is directly or indirectly committed towards supporting the core monetary policy function.

The following are the most common powers granted under central bank statutes for implementing monetary policy:

- determine, alter and abolish reserve requirements;
- buy, sell, issue and discount securities (open market operations);
- grant loans;
- change interest rates and other fees charged to banks for services;
- set quantitative restrictions on bank operations.

Of note is the range of detail regarding legislative provisions in the respective central bank laws. Many laws commit an entire chapter of provisions to monetary policy. But it is also notable, given the central nature of monetary policy, how brief some of the monetary policy provisions are, with very little detail as to the powers or functions delegated and seemingly putting almost no limitations on the pursuit of price and monetary stability. For example, some monetary policy provisions are contained in a single sentence, others in one or two articles, while another simply states that the central bank must act as a central bank.

2. *Foreign exchange and reserves management*

Closely related to, and often intermingled with, legislative provisions regarding monetary policy are provisions granting a central bank authority to engage in foreign exchange and reserves management. Actions undertaken as part of monetary policy, such as a move to alter domestic interest rates, impact the foreign exchange market by changing the foreign exchange value of domestic currency. Thus, a central bank is often granted the authority to conduct both monetary policy and foreign exchange and reserves management to assure a more coordinated effort with regard to currency stability. As in the case of monetary policy, roughly 85 per cent of central banks undertake some form of foreign exchange and reserves management. Alternatively, a number of legal regimes divide the responsibility for these two functions between the central bank (monetary policy) and the ministry of finance or similar branch of government (foreign exchange). The following are the most common grants of authority for engaging in foreign exchange and reserves management under central bank statutes:

- establish, manage and undertake transactions in international/foreign exchange reserves that include precious metals, foreign currency or bank accounts, bills of exchange, debt securities and special drawing rights;

- declare an external value for currency and intervene in the market through purchase or sale of securities or currencies;
- restrict the purchase, sale, holding and transfer of foreign exchange;
- set rules and regulations, primarily by setting limits on positions governing foreign exchange operations;
- receive foreign borrowings, keeping balances with banks in other countries;
- license, revoke licence and supervise foreign exchange dealers and foreign operations.

3. *Lender of last resort*

The lender of last resort function may be defined as 'discretionary provision of liquidity to a financial institution (or the market as a whole) by the central bank in reaction to an adverse shock that causes an increase in demand for liquidity that cannot be met from an alternative source'. These loans are primarily made with two justifications in mind. One is to prevent an otherwise capital solvent bank from failing simply because of a lack of liquidity. The second is to avoid a run on banks that could potentially spill over from bank to bank. This is in contrast to the lending authority granted to central banks as an instrument of monetary policy or as open bank assistance. The grant of authority in central bank statutes generally does not specify the phrase 'lender of last resort loans', but involves an authority to lend under a defined set of circumstances and under explicit limitations. Roughly 80 per cent of central banks have the explicit authority to act as lender of last resort or have a general authority to lend for a purpose that might include lender of last resort circumstances. The terms of this lending authority vary widely based on the following factors:

- what type of entity is eligible, whether it be commercial banks only or a broader sector of institutions;
- the period of maturity for the facility, whether it be very short term or up to one year where terms are specified;
- the security pledged to support the lending facility;
- the exceptions to the generally stated rules such as less stringent pledging requirements, usually in the case of a systemic financial crisis.

The final point above details a distinction with regard to the functions of central banks. Most central banks are granted the authority to lend to banks or other entities in the role of lender of last resort. However, the various exceptions can transform these lending facilities into a separate function: the authority to undertake open bank assistance. The distinction between these two types of lending is that lender of last resort loans are meant to be to solvent entities, for a short period of time, while open bank assistance is meant to be for insolvent entities for a long period of time, potentially permanently.

4. Supervision and regulation of commercial banks

Central banks also commonly supervise commercial banks. It has been argued that the power to supervise banks can actually enhance the conduct of monetary policy by providing confidential bank supervisory information to increase the quality of decision-making. Recently, however, working against this line of reasoning, many central banks have jettisoned the bank supervision function in favour of supervision by a separate unified supervisor that oversees the full range of banking, securities and insurance entities outside of the central bank, or at minimum a supervisor outside of the central bank. Despite this growing trend, approximately 75 per cent of central banks are still involved in commercial bank supervision. The grant of authority in central bank statutes regarding supervision and regulation of commercial banks generally includes the power to:

- license, revoke licences and determine insolvency of commercial banks;
- supervise commercial banks, including examination authority;
- issue rules and regulations regarding banking activities, including issuance of mandatory normatives;
- enforce penalties or take other action for violations of rules and regulations;
- give consent to acquire a controlling interest in a bank;
- establish and maintain an information network for the banking system;
- collect data regarding money laundering for use by a financial intelligence unit external to the central bank.

5. Payments and settlement systems

Central banks are also generally involved in payments and settlement systems, either as participants or as supervisors. The link with monetary policy is that the financial system requires a smooth functioning of the payment system between participating parties, especially in the case of large value payments between banks. A payments system is really any means by which two parties transfer funds to one another. In this sense, currency is one form of payments system. Roughly 80 per cent of central banks are involved in payments and settlement operations. The payments and settlement activities referred to here are of two types: large value payments and small value payments. Large value payments are generally those between banks and constitute the bulk of the total value of payments. Often these payments are handled by central banks. Small value payments are generally made by consumers by means of debit cards, credit cards, automated clearing houses and cheques, and constitute the bulk of the total number of payments. Many of these operations are handled by private entities. The grant of authority in central bank statutes regarding payments and settlement systems generally includes the following powers:

- regulate and conduct interbank clearing;
- arrange for final settlement of interbank payment transactions;
- provide a clearing house for settlement of claims;
- regulate and license settlement and payments system operators and participants (non-interbank);
- perform international payments operations;
- own shares in firms engaged in payments systems.

6. *Currency and coin management*

Central banks also assume responsibility for assuring that sufficient currency and coin are in circulation in the economy. Currency and coin constitute one of the components of the monetary aggregates. This function is primarily administrative, as most issues regarding overall level of money stock are accomplished through setting of monetary policy. Although it is largely an administrative function, the lengthiest provisions in central bank laws are sometimes related to currency operations. Nearly all central banks are responsible for currency operations in some form, as even those central banks without their own currency may have some responsibilities in the area of assuring a regular supply of notes. The grant of authority in central bank statutes regarding currency operations generally includes the following powers and responsibilities:

- define the monetary unit as legal tender, set denominations and grant the central bank monopoly authority to issue;
- assure a regular supply of banknotes and coins;
- sequester and confiscate counterfeited banknotes;

- arrange for security, safekeeping, transportation and storage of issued and unissued banknotes and coins;
- determine amount and procedures for printing banknotes, including type of paper, dimensions;
- exchange banknotes;
- destroy worn notes;
- revoke from circulation any currency and issue a new currency.

7. *Fiscal agent*

Central banks also take on a role as fiscal agent for the government. Fiscal policy and monetary policy are two primary means a government employs to intervene in an economy and the two are often coordinated by delegating some or all of the authority for fiscal matters to the central bank. Approximately 75 per cent of central banks undertake some role as fiscal agent for the government. This role is often shared with the ministry of finance or equivalent department, but the degree of sharing of this role varies widely. The grant of authority in central bank statutes regarding fiscal activities generally includes the following powers and responsibilities:

- represent government in banking relationships, including with foreign states, banks and institutions;
- act as agent for the government in trading securities, including marketing, payment of principal and interest, allocation, registration and transfer;
- grant credit or financial assistance to the government or state agencies for specified maturity, interest rate, limited to a percentage of government revenue;
- act in an advisory capacity on fiscal matters, primarily as related to monetary impact.

Central bank non-core functions

There are a number of other duties for which central banks are responsible that are non-core in the sense that only a small number of central banks undertake them. There does not appear to be a direct link between these functions and the objective of maintaining price and monetary stability. Many of these activities are meant to be temporary in nature: for example, developing a credit bureau or engaging in mortgage activities, with the expectation of passing the activity to private sector operators once the institution is sufficiently developed and financially independent. The following list of functions does not include activities that are an integral part of the previously discussed core functions.

1. *Non-bank financial institution supervision*

The most common activity outside the existing core functions that central banks undertake is the supervision and regulation of non-bank financial institutions. Approximately one-third of central banks supervise some form of non-bank financial institutions. This supervisory authority is closely linked with the bank supervision core function, although in the case of non-bank credit institutions, such as credit unions and savings associations, the institutions supervised are generally smaller in terms of asset size and often do not accept deposits from the general public. Considering the lack of expertise in ministries in the areas of supervision and regulation, I strongly opt for giving to the Central Bank of the Congo the mandate for the supervision and regulation of non-bank financial institutions, including insurance, leasing, social security or pension funds systems, venture capital, financial brokers and dealers, and factoring.

2. *Management of deposit insurance system*

Another relatively common activity for central banks is undertaking some role in the management of a deposit insurance system; approximately 15 per cent of central banks undertake this activity. This involvement takes the form of control of the deposit insurance fund, supervision of the deposit insurance system, operation within the central bank, or management and settlement of the details of coverage for the deposit insurance fund and system. Again, I opt for this responsibility to be assumed by the Central Bank of the Congo due to the relatively small size of the financial system in the Democratic Republic of the Congo and the need to achieve efficiency, synergy and economies of scale in the delivery of services.

3. *Other activities*

The other activities are undertaken by only a small percentage of central banks. Most involve some form of activity related to the activities of banks, such as:

- unified supervisor of financial institutions;
- resolution and liquidation of failing banks;
- financial intelligence unit for anti-money laundering;
- credit bureau;

- mortgage or housing activity;
- open bank assistance;
- agricultural related activity;
- small and medium enterprise loans;
- development banking;
- financial institutions development fund;
- loan to non-banks (corporations);
- export credit;
- ownership of a bank or state bank/loan activity; and
- consumer protection.

For the same reasons given above, the Central Bank of the Congo may be asked to assume some of these duties with a view to transferring them out once the size of the market justifies it and opportunities arise.

Building the credibility of central banks in emerging economies

Central banks should play a key role in policy-making, aiming to promote monetary stability and striving to develop a sound financial sector. Together with governments pursuing prudent macro policies, central banks have all the necessary tools to build the foundation for sustainable long-term economic growth.

The devastating 1997 Asian crisis had a domino effect on other major world regions, bringing important implications for the behaviour of the central banks going forward. A variety of factors led to the financial crisis in Asia. The single largest was, arguably, the inconsistency of macroeconomic policies pursued by the authorities that resulted in elevated levels of external and fiscal deficits, which was also accentuated by a highly indebted corporate sector. Large capital inflows into a fixed exchange rate system were followed neither by tighter fiscal policies nor by central banks' sterilizations. Moreover, the authorities' lack of credibility only added fuel to the currency crisis.

For any central bank, crises create a tremendous opportunity for management to exercise its leadership in implementing the necessary changes. For a number of central banks, successful changes varied with the quality of their leadership (see Chapter 7). Since the Asian crisis, the behavioural pattern of many central banks has changed profoundly. Nowadays, the monetary authorities are more independent, market savvy, credible and transparent. Most importantly, many emerging economies have shifted away from a fixed exchange rate regime to a floating one, which entails active central bank interventions to prevent undesirable currency volatility. The latter often undermines their hard-won credibility and jeopardizes prospects for long-term investments necessary to spur economic growth.

Age-old fears of rising inflation and money supply were somewhat eased with the increasing credibility of the monetary authorities in fighting inflation expectations under the regime of inflation targeting. The major goal of many central banks in emerging economies is to maintain price stability, and monetary policy is the key instrument to achieve lower inflation over time. The central banks seemed to take advantage of large capital inflows into the floating exchange rate regimes to build international reserves through active foreign exchange market interventions while not setting any predetermined currency levels. Higher reserves have been used to buy back external debt which improves a country's macro profile and helps to manage the debt more efficiently. As a result, external vulnerability has been reduced substantially, leading to much more stable markets and prices.

Governments are well aware of debt dynamics and the benefits of fiscal austerity. The budget primary surplus levels are specifically set up in order to stabilize and reduce the debt ratios. In addition, an adequate institutional framework, prudent rules and supervisory standards are all important steps to improve credibility and attract more investments.

Undoubtedly, a lot has been done in the emerging economies since the Asian crisis. The authorities in the emerging economies have learned from past mistakes and are trying hard to take all the necessary measures to defend themselves from global market turbulence. However, a lot still needs to be done in many emerging economies and central banks. Commodity-dependent countries such as the African countries should build a cushion in preparation for periods when the international bonanza reverses. Anti-cyclical funds should be set up to keep the oil or other mining revenues windfall for a rainy day instead of wasting them on higher public sector payrolls. Reforms are still needed in many emerging economies to bring more efficiency, fiscal flexibility, and a faster judicial and administrative response. The credible central banks' floating exchange rate and inflation targeting mechanism, as well as governments' promotion of reforms and fiscal austerity, are all necessary elements to achieve sustainable long-term growth.

Reinventing the Central Bank of the Congo

To be credible, the Central Bank of the Congo must urgently undertake a wide-ranging restructuring and re-engineering effort aimed at the improvement of its processes with a view towards making the bank more efficient and proactive in service delivery. The programme may be given the name LEAGIES to represent the key issues of the project in improving leadership, effectiveness, accountability, goal orientation, independence, efficiency and staff. The overall goals of the project ought to be to address strategic issues, to achieve a sharper focus on core functions of the Central Bank of the Congo and to place the bank in a world-class position with regard to best practices. Project LEAGIES of the Central Bank of the Congo can be undertaken in three phases:

- diagnostic;
- process redesign; and
- implementation.

The project would focus on:

- definition of the core business processes of the BCC;
- rationalization of the processes;
- design of an appropriate operational structure;
- design of an efficient workflow process with checks and balances;
- definition of appropriate IT support; and
- optimum use of skills.

The IT aspects of the project would focus on an enterprise resource planning (ERP) system, real-time gross settlement system (RTGS), banking operations and infrastructure development with emphasis on website development, infrastructure and communications. The project would be embarked upon due to the need to change the entire structure of the BCC with a focus on imbibing a strong culture change using modern information technology as a springboard. It would be intended to radically alter the way things are presently done, including work communication and relationships both within and outside the bank, which means making significant technological changes that pervade the BCC.

The BCC should plan to eliminate in-house responsibilities for a number of its functions and allow private firms to undertake them, including transporting and processing of cash, large-scale investigations of banks, direct trading in the foreign exchange market, security of its premises, clearing and clerical jobs, telecommunications and clearing of cheques and other instruments.

Information technology reforms

The Central Bank of the Congo has to accelerate the upgrading of its IT capability and move forward with the ERP and RTGS software; it also needs a wide area network development and funds transfer. Capabilities for the bank information system must also include identification of methods and patterns used to commit financial crimes.

Other activities

The Central Bank of the Congo must also move forward with the following activities:

- creation of a Development Finance Department to focus on the country's development issues;
- review of the structure of the branches of the Central Bank of the Congo;
- review of the procurement process; and
- creation of a performance improvement department.

Based on recent organizational audits of the Central Bank of the Congo, the organization structure needs to adopt a new department structure concentrating mainly on the four core mandates of the central bank which include issuance and management of legal tender currency; management of the nation's external reserves; promotion of monetary stability and a sound financial system; as well as operating as banker and financial adviser to the government. This is important because for the time being about 60 per cent of the departments are geared towards non-core functions.

Cultural sensitivity and quality people

Cultural legitimacy is the final and most important issue to confront in restructuring the Central Bank of the Congo. What foreigners write or say is irrelevant unless the people of the Democratic Republic of the Congo are involved. Most importantly, nobody from abroad should be allowed to go into the Democratic Republic of the Congo and build a set of institutions that reflect American and Western European values. This would not work. The Central Bank of the Congo belongs to the Congolese people and they have to build it up themselves. As part of the central bank reform, it is fitting to start thinking about printing a new reformed Congolese currency to replace the outdated and worthless current currency notes. This would be, in addition to the new fiscal conservatism and the government institutions that are in place, a positive step towards the end of dollarization. And while I might think that publication of a quarterly report on inflation conditions is a good way for central bankers to communicate with the public and ensure accountability, if the people of the

Democratic Republic of the Congo want to do it differently, that is their prerogative.

The international community can contribute to setting up a comprehensive framework of principles that are universal and that are applicable to central banks worldwide, but the details must be left up to the people of the Democratic Republic of the Congo. The quality of people both in the Central Bank's top management and the entire hierarchy will ultimately determine the value and credibility of the institution. There must be no substitute for highly educated and trained staff throughout the entire institution while continuous education and professional training programmes would help to keep their skills up-to-date.

Conclusion

The task of maintaining price and monetary stability, the most common objective of central banks, is an immense task. We need to reject the idea that all the functions that a central bank in an emerging democracy currently performs in meeting this objective are necessarily those it should continue to perform as it moves forward. Achieving efficiency of operations dictates that a credible central bank performs only those underlying functions necessary to achieve this objective. Those central banks that have undertaken a detailed review of their operations in an effort to improve the efficiency of their operations, many of which are detailed in this book, should be lauded for taking on such a challenging task.

If the Congolese people wish to achieve what the Germans or the Americans have in setting up the Bundesbank and the Federal Reserve System, or what the Europeans have done in setting up the European Central Bank, then there is no alternative but to transform the Central Bank of the Congo into a powerful and credible central bank. Their currency could then become as strong as the euro or the dollar.

5
A Strategic Vision for the Financial Sector

A large body of evidence now exists which shows that financial sector development can make an important contribution to economic growth and poverty reduction. This is especially true in the Democratic Republic of the Congo, whose financial sector is particularly underdeveloped, and without it economic development would certainly be constrained even if other necessary conditions are met. Insufficient financial development may leave the Democratic Republic of the Congo in a 'poverty trap'. Because of increasing returns to scale in the financial sector, a vicious circle can be created, where low levels of financial intermediation result in only a few market players. The lack of competition results in high costs, leading to low real deposit rates and hence low savings, which in turn limits the amount of financial intermediation. Financial sector underdevelopment can therefore be a serious obstacle to growth in the Democratic Republic of the Congo, even when the country has established other conditions necessary for sustained economic development such as the rule of law, solid democratic institutions, economic and social infrastructure, lasting peace, and human capital.

By increasing the savings rate and the availability of savings for investment, facilitating and encouraging inflows of foreign capital, and optimizing the allocation of capital between competing uses, financial sector development can boost long-run growth through its impact on capital accumulation and on the rate of technological progress. Though the scale may be different, access to financial services can reduce poverty through the same channels that affect overall growth: by increasing investment and productivity resulting in greater income generation, and by facilitating risk management thus reducing vulnerability to shocks. However, poor people in the Democratic Republic of the Congo often do not have access to ongoing, formal financial services, and are forced to rely instead on a narrow range of highly risky and expensive informal services. This constrains their ability to participate fully in markets, to increase their incomes and to contribute to the economic growth of the country.

In the Democratic Republic of the Congo, semi-formal channels such as microfinance institutions have began to play a role in providing financial services to the poor, as do institutions such as traditional commercial banks. But these institutions reach only a minority of the bankable population in a country where the banking penetration rate is just 0.5 per cent. So a widening of financial services provision by different private and public sector institutions (such as commercial banks, merchant banks, venture capital, factoring, leasing, brokers, development institutions and other specialized banks) in the formal financial sector is necessary to tackle this problem on an adequate scale.

Such a development requires a new focus on ways to encourage, and remove barriers to, wider formal financial sector provision of services. It also requires that the Congolese people completely rethink the structure and functioning of the overall financial system in the Democratic Republic of the Congo to meet the needs, not of the colonial patrons, but of a truly independent country and its population. This also implies that, when designing regulatory reform (for example to promote stability or security), greater attention needs to be paid to the incentives and regulatory space that private sector financial institutions have to widen access. Better data on access to financial services are also required, in order to understand the development needs of the country, identify the barriers to wider formal sector provision, identify the kind of institutions that are needed and that can make the difference, and motivate the government and the private sector to take action to support the development of the financial sector and facilitate wider access by contributing to the implementation of well-understood action plans. This is the purpose of the strategic vision for the financial sector of the Democratic Republic of the Congo, which proposes a new structure for the Congolese financial and banking system to address in a lasting and sustainable manner the development challenges of the country and its people.

Developing the financial sector of the Democratic Republic of the Congo cannot be achieved accidentally. It must be planned and the plan must be carefully implemented over time. One has first to visualize the type of system that the Democratic Republic of the Congo needs for its development before that system can be implemented. Because the current system is known to be insufficient, inadequate and out of date, I propose the following strategic agenda for the development of the financial sector in the Democratic Republic of the Congo.

THE REGULATORY AUTHORITIES

- The Ministry of Finance
- The Central Bank of the Congo
- The Congo Deposit Insurance Corporation
- The Congo Securities and Exchange Commission
- The National Insurance Commission
- The National Mortgage Bank of the Congo
- The Financial Services Coordinating Committee

THE MONEY MARKET AND ITS INSTITUTIONS

- Discount houses
- Commercial and merchant banks
- Microfinance institutions

THE CAPITAL MARKET

- The Kinshasa Stock Exchange
- The primary market
- The secondary market
- The unit trust scheme

DEVELOPMENT FINANCE INSTITUTIONS

- The International Bank for the Reconstruction and Development of the Congo
- The Congolese Industrial Development Bank
- The Congolese Bank for Commerce and Industry
- The Congolese Agricultural and Cooperative Bank
- The Urban Development Bank

OTHER FINANCIAL INSTITUTIONS AND FUNDS

- Insurance companies
- Finance, leasing, factoring and venture capital companies
- Bureaux de change
- Primary mortgage institutions

- The Industrial Promotion Fund
- The Congolese Social Insurance Trust Fund
- The National Social Security Institute

The regulatory authorities

There is a wide-ranging plan to overhaul the financial services industry, aiming to improve the regulation of the financial system and to promote the development of new institutions. The current Congolese regulatory framework was born out of the colonial era and is not well suited for today's environment. The new proposal covers all aspects of the financial services industry, including insurance companies, securities firms, commercial and investment banks as well as financial and capital markets. It represents a broad structural shift in the promotion, development and regulation of financial firms, both reshaping the central bank oversight in some instances and expanding the government's regulatory role in areas such as insurance, leasing, mortgages, investment banking, capital markets and financial markets.

The proposed blueprint envisions consolidation and strengthening of the oversight function, initially under the central bank only, and later under two regulators. The BCC, with a broad authority to examine firms, would likely serve as a market stability regulator. In the long run, the supervision function would be transferred to a 'Prudent Financial Regulator' that will be mandated to oversee commercial banks, investment banks, insurance companies, leasing, and venture capital. It would also regulate business conduct, including consumer protection. I favour a single regulator inside or outside the Central Bank of the Congo rather than two separate entities. The proposed plan will expand the power of the BCC over non-bank financial institutions. At this stage in the development of the Congo there is a great need for a separate mortgage supervisory agent to ensure that sufficient residential mortgage loans are available to Congolese consumers. The ongoing housing crisis in the US shows the importance of supporting mortgage banks and other traditional home lenders over the non-bank mortgage lenders that played a major role in causing the current turmoil. While the proposed CDIC would be a separate entity from the Central Bank of the Congo, it is to be hoped that economies of scale would be achieved by maintaining a joint supervision function under the auspices of the BCC.

The Congolese financial system is to be restructured and redesigned to comprise bank and non-bank financial institutions which would be regulated by the Ministry of Finance (MF), the Central Bank of Congo

(BCC), the Congo Deposit Insurance Corporation (CDIC), the Congo Securities and Exchange Commission (CSEC), the National Insurance Commission (NIC), the National Mortgage Bank of the Congo (NMBC), and the National Board for Community Banks (NBCB). The BCC would introduce legislation that would allow the operation of more banks from other countries on a reciprocal basis. The Central Bank of the Congo would also consider allowing foreign banks operating in the Congo to set up new branches provided that they undertake to employ Congolese nationals and to limit the number of expatriate staff to no more than two to three for the institution.

The Ministry of Finance

The Ministry of Finance advises the central government on its fiscal operation and cooperates with the BCC on monetary matters. Recent amendment to the laws of the Central Bank of Congo compels the BCC to maintain a relationship with the rest of the government and with the executive branch through the Ministry of Finance.

The Central Bank of the Congo

The BCC is the apex regulatory authority of the financial system. It was re-established in its current configuration by the Central Bank of the Congo Act of 2002 (although the central bank was created in 1961). Among its primary functions, the Bank promotes monetary stability and a sound financial system, and acts as banker and financial adviser to the central government, as well as banker of last resort to the banks. The Central Bank of the Congo also encourages the growth and development of financial institutions. In 2002, enabling laws gave the Central Bank of the Congo more flexibility in regulating and overseeing the banking sector and licensing microfinance companies which hitherto operated outside any regulatory framework. The Bank's performance over the last ten years (as measured by an average inflation rate of 139 per cent per year) has raised questions as to its institutional autonomy and effectiveness in the conduct of monetary policy.

To ensure credibility and performance effectiveness, the Central Bank of the Congo would be restructured and reorganized along a decentralized model including four financial districts, a National Open Market Committee (or a Monetary Policy Committee) and a Board of Governors. This would be consistent with the recent decentralization of the administrative functions following the advent of the third Republic. The restructuring agenda of the Central Bank would also entail (i) the revision of the Central Bank Law to grant more independence to the monetary authority and to make the Central Bank more accountable; (ii) a human resource development programme; (iii) the development of appropriate instruments to meet the Bank's mandated objectives; (iv) a comprehensive monetary reform that would bring more credibility to the local currency and contribute to ending the widespread dollarization; (v) the rehabilitation of the physical infrastructures and the payments system; (vi) the reorganization of the Central Bank departments along its primary mandate; and (vii) the restructuring of the currency printing shop to make it more cost effective and efficient.

The Congo Deposit Insurance Corporation

The recommendation for the Democratic Republic of the Congo to have a deposit insurance scheme is based on the peculiarities and widely recognized roles that a stable banking system can play in the economic development of the country. Deposit-taking financial institutions serve as intermediaries between the surplus and deficit units of the economy. These institutions are not only the lifeblood that sustains the economic development process, but also play the distinctive role of bearing all of the risks associated with the economic system. The intermediation process essentially entails risk-taking, with the risks taking on different forms: operational, liquidity, reputational, etc.

Because the operations of financial institutions affect all stakeholders including the general public, there is no government in the world that does not utilize various means, both direct and indirect, to minimize any damage that might be inflicted on the rights and interests of depositors as a result of failure of financial institutions. In the past, by closely supervising financial institutions and maintaining strict controls over the scope of their business operations, the government of the Democratic Republic of the Congo had implicitly safeguarded the depositors' funds. More recently, however, many countries (see Appendix 1) have adopted deposit insurance or guaranteed deposit systems with a view to explicitly safeguarding the rights and interests of depositors, especially small ones. A deposit insurance scheme is a financial guarantee to protect depositors, particularly the small ones, in the event of a bank failure. By this means, confidence in the banking system is engendered and the stability of the system facilitated. Deposit insurance serves as one of the complementary measures employed by the monetary authority for effective management and orderly resolution of problems associated with both failing and failed deposit-taking financial institutions. The scheme provides government with a framework for intervention and sterilization of the disruptive effects on the economy of failures of deposit-taking institutions.

Without a deposit insurance system, the Democratic Republic of the Congo, like many countries, particularly in Africa, has extended implicit deposit protection to depositors on a discretionary ad hoc basis. Explicit deposit insurance systems have several advantages over these implicit protection schemes. By replacing discretion with rules, explicit deposit insurance provides a faster, smoother and more consistent administrative process for extending protection to depositors and for protection against bank runs. Although there are arguments against deposit insurance schemes, on balance the merits outweigh the demerits and therefore, it is surprising that such a scheme has not yet been established in the Democratic Republic of the Congo.

Explicit deposit insurance schemes have a great potential for enhancing the effectiveness of the Democratic Republic of the Congo's financial system. This section focuses on the concept of deposit insurance; the potential roles of a deposit insurance scheme; the relevance and desirability of deposit insurance in the Congo; and experiences from some countries with explicit deposit insurance in place. It is hoped that this discussion will go a long way to highlight the importance of this unique scheme that could make a great difference in the way the public assesses the usefulness and safety of the financial system. It is also hoped that emphasizing the importance of this issue will encourage the Democratic Republic of the Congo to embrace the scheme.

The concept of deposit insurance

A deposit insurance scheme (DIS) is 'a mutual insurance system supported by insured banks and administered either through a government controlled agency or a privately held one' (FresFalex, 1991). The agency guarantees deposits in the insured institutions and stands ready to reimburse depositors promptly in the event of the insured bank's failure. Deposit insurance schemes developed as a result of the need to provide some form of protection to depositors who stood the risk of losing their hard-earned money in the event of bank failures. Coupled with this was the need to insulate the banking system from instability that could result from bank runs and loss of depositors' confidence. The practice of deposit insurance differs from one jurisdiction to another. Over the years, however, some best practices have emerged to guide countries that have established deposit insurance schemes or countries wishing to create one. Essentially, the practices of deposit insurance schemes deal with the issues of ownership and administration, membership, funding, coverage, pricing and failure resolution. All these features have been extensively discussed in the literature.

Deposit insurance was first introduced by some states in the US in the 1840s. However, Norway was the first country to establish a nationwide DIS for its savings and commercial banks in 1921 and 1938 respectively. Finland and the former Czechoslovakia established theirs in 1924 while the nationwide scheme in the US was established in 1933 following the Great Depression of that year. In Canada, a compulsory DIS was adopted in 1967 (Laeven, 2004). In Asia, India was the first country with a deposit insurance scheme in 1961, followed by the Philippines in 1963. In Africa, the first scheme was established in Kenya in 1985, followed by the Nigerian scheme in 1988.

Deposit insurance differs from general forms of conventional insurance. Commercial insurance, on the one hand, is profit-oriented and only serves to safeguard the property of an individual. Deposit insurance, on the other hand, is a safety net vehicle designed to stabilize financial systems and safeguard the rights and interests of depositors in financial institutions by encouraging cooperation between the government and businesses in relation to the provision of credit. It is not profit-oriented. In addition, deposit insurance serves to guard against financial loss to an appropriate degree.

In other words, deposit insurance does not passively wait for a catastrophe to happen before providing compensation, but adopts all kinds of preventive measures to promote sound operations of insured institutions. This is where deposit insurance and commercial insurance in general fundamentally differ. There are basically two types of deposit insurance schemes. There are *implicit deposit insurance schemes* and *explicit deposit insurance schemes*. The implicit form is a discretionary approach adopted by government to prop up some failing deposit-taking institutions in the absence of an explicit statutory obligation on the part of government to protect depositors. The government is therefore at liberty to decide whether or not to grant any relief to depositors and the amount of such relief. This is the kind of system that currently prevails in the Democratic Republic of the Congo. The approach is not desirable because it creates uncertainty in the minds of depositors which in turn can intensify runs on other banks.

An explicit deposit insurance scheme is created by a legal instrument. The enabling statute usually states the objectives of the scheme and other operational guidelines relating to issues such as ownership, funding, extent of coverage, membership, supervisory and resolution powers, and others. Specifically, an explicit deposit insurance scheme provides a formal framework with clear-cut rules and procedures for providing protection to depositors as well as for assessment and management of failed and failing deposit-taking institutions. An explicit deposit insurance scheme can be designed as a 'risk minimizer' or as a 'paybox'. It is logical for the administrator of the deposit insurance scheme to want to know and to minimize the extent of risk it is exposed to and to monitor the changes in the composition and extent of such risk through close supervision of the insured institution. This is the risk minimization responsibility of the deposit insurer. For effectiveness, the statute establishing the scheme in countries where risk minimization is the focus of the deposit insurance scheme usually provides powers for supervision to the deposit insurer. In many cases, such powers cover onsite examination and offsite surveillance of insured institutions.

Offsite supervision involves the receipt and analysis of periodic statutory returns from insured institutions to ascertain compliance with prudential standards and other regulations, whereas the focus and scope of bank examination are dictated by the perceived levels of risk posed by the insured institution to the insurance fund. In developing countries, including the Democratic Republic of the Congo, where the quality of information supplied by financial institutions is generally low, onsite examination becomes a relevant tool to confirm the accuracy of information contained in bank returns. In some countries, however, the deposit insurer is not empowered to supervise insured institutions; instead the deposit insurance scheme in such jurisdictions operates as a paybox, i.e. it pays insured depositors in the event of a bank failure. In several African countries, the deposit insurance scheme is designed as a paybox.

The potential roles of a deposit insurance scheme

The decision to establish a deposit insurance scheme is usually influenced by the potential roles of the scheme. Some of these roles include the following.

1. Protection for unsophisticated depositors. The less financially sophisticated depositors are often distinguished by the small size of their deposits. These classes of depositors are singled out for protection because they do not have the means and/or capability of carrying out the complex task of monitoring and assessing the condition of their financial institutions. This is often not the case with financially sophisticated depositors with a large volume of deposits. A deposit insurance scheme can therefore be put in place in the Democratic Republic of the Congo to address the inequity that exists between financially sophisticated and unsophisticated depositors. This is even more necessary because the majority of the Congolese population is not financially sophisticated enough to be able to read and analyse a bank balance sheet to assess the inherent risks associated with the institution.

Proponents of deposit insurance such as myself argue that it is neither reasonable nor fair to expect unsophisticated individuals to monitor banks whose portfolios of assets consist largely of loans. The costs of monitoring a bank for small depositors may outweigh the benefits and therefore it may be rational for them to not actively monitor the condition of their banks. Instead, ignorant small depositors will seek to protect their interests by withdrawing their deposits whenever they are presented with information that causes them to question the solvency of their banks, i.e. they will run on their banks. Their ignorance may also prevent them from distinguishing between good information on the condition of their depository institution and false rumours; hence, they may participate in runs on solvent banks. It is, however, important to know that although a deposit insurance scheme protects depositors against the consequences associated with the failure of an insured institution, it is not designed to protect banks and/or any other deposit-taking financial institution from failing. For a country with a very low banking penetration rate of 0.5 per cent, a deposit insurance scheme would be necessary to convince the sceptical public to deposit their money in a financial institution in the first place. A good deposit insurance scheme combined with a strong campaign by its authorities as well as the central bank and the government, can considerably contribute to increasing the banking penetration rate throughout the country.

2. Promoting confidence in, and stability of, the banking system. This objective is based on a concern that depositors may lose confidence in an institution under certain circumstances. A well-designed deposit insurance scheme would contribute to the stability of the Democratic Republic of the Congo's financial system. A protected depositor is not likely to be a panicky one at the first sign of a problem in his or her bank. If depositors do not rush to withdraw their deposits and in the process precipitate a run on their bank and contagiously on other banks, banking stability in the Democratic Republic of the Congo is more likely to be maintained. A deposit insurance scheme may also attract more business for banking institutions in the Democratic Republic of the Congo by increasing the number of their potential depositors.

3. Other deposit insurance roles. In addition to the provision of deposit protection for less financially sophisticated depositors and a contribution to financial stability by promoting confidence in the banking system, a deposit insurance scheme can also be designed to play the following roles in the Democratic Republic of the Congo.

(a) *A formal mechanism for dealing with problem financial institutions.* A deposit insurance scheme, in conjunction with the Central Bank of the Congo, may provide the Congolese government with a formalized mechanism for dealing with problem financial institutions with a view to protecting depositors. The introduction of a deposit insurance system may be linked to the Democratic Republic of the Congo's attempt to put in place laws and mechanisms that deal with failed institutions. Experience suggests that the failure of depository institutions must be handled in unique ways to deal with the tendency of troubled institutions to deteriorate rapidly, while minimizing adverse effects on the overall financial system. The introduction of deposit insurance may be linked to the creation of a country's failure-resolution framework for its deposit-taking financial institutions.
(b) *Contributing to an orderly payment system.* Deposit insurance in the Democratic Republic of the Congo can help to promote financial stability by contributing to the smooth functioning of the payments system. Depository institutions allow individuals and businesses to save and withdraw money when it is needed. By promoting confidence in the Congolese financial system, deposit insurance would facilitate the smooth transfer of deposits between parties. Some deposit insurance systems are also able to provide a form of short-term financial assistance, which may involve guaranteeing the payment obligations of troubled institutions. Such assistance may help to avoid interruptions in payment and settlement flows. In so doing, such assistance provides time for safety net participants to devise long-term solutions to resolve troubled institutions.
(c) *Transition from full to limited coverage.* The Democratic Republic of the Congo may introduce an explicit, limited coverage deposit insurance system as a way of facilitating the transition away from the current ineffective full deposit guarantee provided by the government. The DRC's current theoretical full coverage exists because the public policy objective emphasis is to give the banking system protection against contagious runs.

    Blanket coverage, on the other hand, is usually applied during systemic crisis that threatens the payments system. This occurred when the Banque de Kinshasa ran into trouble in the 1980s and the central bank ended up allowing it to run a huge overdraft on its books to meet the depositors' demands. The overdraft became so big that the only way out was for the central bank to transform its exposure into an equity participation in the Banque de Kinshasa which then changed its name to La Nouvelle Banque de Kinshasa. To transit from full coverage, deposit insurance systems may allow the government of the Democratic Republic of the Congo to reduce coverage, and also provide a mechanism for managing the required change in public and market attitudes towards deposit protection.

The relevance of deposit insurance in the Democratic Republic of the Congo and Africa

Against the myriad social, economic, political and other developmental problems facing the African continent, a pertinent question to ask is whether the deposit insurance objective of protecting depositors, preventing bank runs, sustaining confidence in banks and promoting financial stability is relevant in the Democratic Republic of the Congo in particular, and in Africa in general. The economic literature is replete with studies which find significant contributions of the financial sector to economic development and the primacy of banking in the financial system.

In order to make the needed contributions to development, banks in particular require cash deposits which are their life blood. In the Democratic Republic of the Congo and in many other African economies, banks are the dominant and the most developed entities in the financial system. In the Democratic Republic of the Congo for example, banks' total assets in relation to that of the financial services industry currently stand at over 90 per cent. Whilst there is a clear need for diversification of financial service providers, there is no doubt that banks and other deposit-taking financial institutions should be encouraged to mobilize more savings for development. In such an endeavour, a scheme to protect small savers who provide the bulk of the funds in the Democratic Republic of the Congo deserves consideration and introduction.

Globally, there is ample evidence to show that the presence of an effective deposit insurance scheme to protect depositors engenders confidence in depository institutions, minimizes bank runs and contributes to financial stability. Bank runs are contagious and the most pernicious effect of a panic is that it may result in the closing down of sound financial institutions along with the unsound ones.

One possible major argument against deposit insurance in the Democratic Republic of the Congo is the issue of moral hazard. The problem of moral hazard arises from the distortion in incentives induced by deposit protection. The presence of depositor protection in the Democratic Republic of the Congo could affect the behaviour of the economic agents involved, particularly their willingness to assume greater risk. If deposit insurance is achieved by bailing out banks and their shareholders, shareholders may be subject to moral hazard by betting on the Congolese government's or the insurer's fund. However, if the deposit protection is structured so that shareholders and managers do not benefit from deposit protection, the introduction of this protection in the Democratic Republic of the Congo would not significantly increase the moral hazard of bankers.

To get the full benefit of a deposit insurance scheme, the extent of protection to depositors should be such that it allows the scheme to achieve its objectives without inducing significant moral hazard. Presently, while all African countries license banks and some welcome international banks, only a few countries have established explicit deposit insurance schemes to protect depositors. The countries without explicit deposit protection schemes tend to rely on implicit protection of depositors through bank support to prevent failure. However, the prevention of banking failures is a Herculean task. A well-managed bank can fail because of factors beyond the bank management's control. For example, factors exogenous to the bank such as economic downturn, political upheavals, war and others can bring down a bank. If the deposits of such a bank were not insured, the government would be forced to use taxpayers' money to refund the depositors or, as has been the case in some African countries in the past, including the Democratic Republic of the Congo, the government could allow the depositors to carry their burden alone. There is no doubt that the well-being of nations, particularly developing ones like those in Africa, is critically dependent on economic growth and development which, in turn, significantly depend on the stability of the financial services industry, particularly the banking sub-sector. A stable banking system is likely to guarantee financial stability given the dominance of banks in the financial system in the Democratic Republic of the Congo. In turn, a stable financial system is required for economic stability and development in the Democratic Republic of the Congo, with all the rewards that that will bring.

Having argued the case in favour of a deposit insurance scheme in the Democratic Republic of the Congo, I would like to recommend very strongly that the country establish, as part of a broad strategy for developing the financial sector, a formal deposit insurance scheme. The Congo

Deposit Insurance Corporation (CDIC) would be an independent agency created by the Parliament to maintain the stability of, and public confidence in, the nation's financial system by insuring deposits, examining and supervising financial institutions, and managing receiverships in conjunction with and under the umbrella of the BCC.

The CDIC would be created to complement the regulatory and supervisory role of the BCC. It would, however, be autonomous of the BCC and would report to the Ministry of Finance. The CDIC would be set up to provide deposit insurance and related services for banks in order to promote confidence in the banking industry. The CDIC would be empowered to examine the books and affairs of insured banks and other deposit-taking financial institutions. A depositor's claim would be limited to a maximum of $25,000 in the event of a bank failure. A Deposit Insurance Fund (DIF) would be created and maintained by the CDIC. The CDIC would maintain the DIF by assessing depository institutions as regards their insurance premium.[1] The amount at which each institution would be assessed would be based both on the balance of insured deposits as well as on the degree of risk the institution poses to the insurance fund. On average, licensed banks would be mandated to pay 15/16 of 1 per cent of their total deposit liabilities as insurance premium to the CDIC.

In designing a deposit insurance scheme for the Democratic Republic of the Congo, one has to keep in mind some key features of effective deposit insurance systems that have been developed based on best practices. Despite the variations in deposit insurance systems internationally, experience has shown that there are some general principles that can maximize the effectiveness of deposit insurance in promoting stable banking systems. The specific design features that work best would vary from country to country, but these key challenges always have to be addressed:

- First, the deposit insurance system should function within a suitable legal framework with appropriate accounting rules, prudential bank supervision, and consumer protection.
- Second, the deposit insurance system should be clearly understood by the public. Publiç awareness of the deposit insurance programme is essential for its effectiveness.
- Third, the deposit insurance coverage provided by the system must be adequate to provide assurance to most depositors.
- Fourth, the process for closing banks and promptly paying depositors and other claimants must also be efficient and clearly understood.

- Fifth, the deposit insurer must have access to information on insured institutions as necessary to monitor risk exposure.
- Sixth, most successful deposit insurance programmes include reliable funding sources for timely action in the event of bank failures.
- Seventh, a deposit insurance system should establish standards for institutions to qualify for insurance such as capital, internal controls, and sound risk management.
- Finally, the deposit insurance system should have strong corporate governance.

With the above in mind, I believe that a well-designed system of deposit insurance, coupled with an effective system of prudential bank regulation, are the most effective means of maintaining Congolese public confidence and financial stability during times of stress. As such, a well-designed deposit insurance scheme will contribute significantly to the development of the financial system.

The Congo Securities and Exchange Commission

The Congo Securities and Exchange Commission (CSEC) would be established by a law approved by the Parliament. It would be an apex regulatory organ of the capital market. Its major objective would be the promotion of a transparent, orderly and active capital market. In doing this, the CSEC would have the major functions of ensuring adequate protection of securities; determining the time frame for the sale of company securities; approving the volume of such securities; and registering all securities dealers, investment advisers and market places (such as stock exchange branches) in order to maintain proper standards of conduct and professionalism in the securities business. The Commission would be set up to approve and regulate mergers and acquisitions and authorize the establishment of unit trusts. In the course of deregulation of the capital market, the function of price determination would be transferred to the issuing houses. The CSEC would maintain surveillance over the market to enhance efficiency and issue guidelines on the establishment of stock exchanges in furtherance of the deregulation of the capital market. The CSEC would also release guidelines on foreign investments in the Congolese capital market.

The National Insurance Commission

The National Insurance Commission (NIC) would be created to replace the Congolese Insurance Division within the Ministry of Finance. The

NIC would be charged with effective administration, supervision, regulation and control of the business of insurance in the Democratic Republic of the Congo. Its specific functions would include the establishment of standards for the conduct of insurance business, protection of insurance policy holders, and establishment of a bureau to which complaints might be submitted against insurance companies and their intermediaries by members of the public. The NIC would ensure adequate capitalization and reserves, good management, effective governance, high technical expertise and judicious fund placement in the insurance industry. Initially the supervision of the insurance industry may be assumed by the central bank; it would later be taken over by the NIC once the size of the market justifies it.

The National Mortgage Bank of the Congo

The National Mortgage Bank of the Congo (NMBC) would provide banking and advisory services, and undertake research activities pertaining to housing. Following the adoption of the National Housing Policy by the Parliament (the government and the central bank would have to work with Parliament on this initiative), the NMBC would be empowered to license and regulate primary mortgage institutions in the Democratic Republic of the Congo and act as the apex regulatory body for the mortgage finance industry. The NMBC would retain a regulatory role while a mortgage finance entity would be created by the government in partnership with the private sector to provide housing finance activities. The NMBC would be under the control of the Central Bank of the Congo and the Ministry of Finance.

The Financial Services Coordinating Committee

The Financial Services Coordinating Committee (FSCC) would be a committee established to coordinate the activities of all regulatory institutions in the financial system.

The Committee would be chaired by the governor of the Central Bank of the Congo and would report to the president of the Republic, the prime minister, the president of the National Assembly and the president of the Senate through the minister of finance.

The money market and its institutions

This is a market for short-term debt instruments. The major function of the money market is to facilitate the raising of short-term funds from the surplus sectors to the deficit sectors of the economy. The deficit units, which could be public or private, obtain funds from the market to bridge budgetary gaps by trading in short-term securities such as Treasury Bills, Treasury Certificates, Call Money, Certificates of Deposit (CDs), and Commercial Papers (CP). With the commencement of Open Market Operations (OMO) by the BCC, the scope of the money market would be expanded to include private sector participants over time. The number of participants in the market would also increase with the establishment of discount houses. Money market institutions would constitute the hub of the financial system. These institutions would include discount houses, commercial and merchant banks, and special-purpose banks, like the ProCredit and community banks.

Discount houses

A discount house as a special, non-bank financial institution intervenes in mobilizing funds for investments in securities in response to the liquidity of the system. It does this by providing discount/rediscounting facilities in government short-term securities. In the process of shifting the financial system from direct market-based monetary control, discount houses would be established to serve as financial intermediaries between the BCC, licensed banks and other financial institutions. We would aim at developing at least five discount houses in operation in the Democratic Republic of the Congo within the next five years.

Commercial and merchant banks

Commercial and merchant banks operate under the legal framework of the Banks and Other Financial Institutions Law.

Commercial banks

The first commercial bank established in the Congo was the Banque Commerciale du Congo in 1909. After nearly 100 years of operations, the Banque Commerciale du Congo had assets totalling 185 million dollars as of 31 December 2006: hardly a sign of great success. Commercial banks perform three major functions, namely, acceptance of deposits, granting of loans and the operation of the payments and settlement mechanism. Since the government commenced active deregulation of the economy in September 2002, the commercial banking sector has continued to witness limited growth, especially in terms of the number of institutions and product innovations in the market.

The numbers of commercial banks and their branches were 11 and 43, respectively, in 2006. Many branches are concentrated in Kinshasa. The minimum capitalization of both commercial and merchant banks has been increased to a uniform level of $3 million. The commercial banks continue to dominate the banking sector, accounting for 95 per cent of the banking system's total assets and deposit liabilities in 2006. The total assets of the commercial banks increased to $778 million at the end of 2006. This is a very small banking sector considering the size of the country (2,342,000 square kilometres and a population of 62 million) and its development needs.

Merchant banks

Merchant banks take deposits and cater for the needs of corporate and institutional customers by way of providing short-, medium- and long-term loan financing, and engaging in activities such as equipment leasing, loan syndication, debt factoring and project advisers to clients sourcing funds in the market. The Democratic Republic of the Congo has yet to establish its first merchant bank. The Central Bank of the Congo and the government should pursue an active policy to promote these institutions.

Microfinance institutions

The decision to establish the ProCredit bank specializing in microfinance was announced by the government in 2004. Specifically, the bank is to meet the credit needs of small borrowers who cannot satisfy the stringent collateral requirements normally demanded by commercial banks. The bank is expected to facilitate access to credit for urban, poor, small-scale operators and thereby increase their self-reliance. The lending floor and ceiling have been removed and applications are treated on their individual merits. But ProCredit is a small institution in a country where the majority of the population can be considered microfinance potential customers. There is a need to better organize this sector and give it the necessary support by encouraging the emergence of several other institutions similar to ProCredit across the country.

The capital market

Developing the Congolese capital market is a matter of priority and urgency. The Congolese capital market would be a channel for mobilizing long-term funds. The main institutions in the market would include the Congo Securities and Exchange Commission (CSEC), which would be at the apex and serve as the regulatory authority of the securities market, the Kinshasa Stock Exchange (KSE), which must be created urgently, the issuing houses and the stock broking firms. The capital market would be classified into primary and secondary segments.

The Kinshasa Stock Exchange

The Democratic Republic of the Congo should aim to launch the Kinshasa Stock Exchange (KSE) within the next three years. To encourage small as well as large-scale enterprises' access to public listing, the KSE would operate the main exchange for relatively large enterprises, and for small and medium-scale enterprises. Listing requirements for small and medium enterprises would be made less stringent to facilitate their participation in the market. Indications should be given to the public as to what requirements have been relaxed to facilitate the listing of small and medium-sized enterprises.

The primary market

A primary market is a market for new issues of securities. The mode of offer for the securities traded in this market would include offer for subscription, rights issues, offer for sale and private placements. In aggregate, the Congo should aim to have a minimum of forty issues within the first five years.

The secondary market

This is a market for trading in existing securities. This would consist of exchange and over-the-counter markets where securities are bought and sold after their issuance in the primary market. The aim should be to have at least four trading floors in the Democratic Republic of the Congo (Kinshasa, Lubumbashi, Mbuji Mayi and Kisangani) during the first five years. The number of stock brokers trading on the Exchange would be limited to fifty companies to ensure quality at entry and develop trust in the market. We would aim to have a market capitalization of at least $5 billion in the first ten years.

The unit trust scheme

This is a mechanism for mobilizing the financial resources of small and big savers, and managing such funds to achieve maximum returns with minimum risks through efficient portfolio diversification. Unit trusts should be launched at the same time as the KSE and other capital market instruments.

Development finance institutions

Specialized banks or development finance institutions (DFIs) would be established to contribute to the development of specific sectors of the economy. They would consist of the International Bank for the Reconstruction and Development of the Congo (IBRDC), the Congo Industrial Development Bank (CIDB), the Congo Bank for Commerce and Industry (CBCI), the Congo Agricultural and Cooperative Bank (CACB), and the Urban Development Bank (UDB). Like other financial institutions, all development banks would be under the supervision of the Central Bank of the Congo.

The International Bank for the Reconstruction and Development of the Congo

Considering that the country's economy and infrastructure have been seriously impacted by years of mismanagement and corrupt practices, there is a need to channel the efforts, energies and resources in an efficient manner towards well thought out actions, projects and programmes for sustainable development. I suggest that the Democratic Republic of the Congo set up a development institution or development bank, called, for example, the International Bank for the Reconstruction and Development of the Congo (IBRDC).

The IBRDC would be owned by the Democratic Republic of the Congo, development funds, and key donor countries and institutions interested in the development of the Congo. Subscriptions to the capital would be without restrictions and donor countries, institutions and development funds would be welcomed and encouraged. However, control over the decision-making process should remain in Congolese hands so that the Congolese people are responsible for their country's destiny in conformity with its national sovereignty. This is possible through a system of Tier I and Tier II capital or the equivalent system of shares A and B with different voting privileges. Other shareholders' views would be protected through sufficient representation on the Board of Executive Directors.

The purpose of the bank would be to mobilize financial resources and utilize them to finance development projects throughout the Democratic Republic of the Congo so as to ensure a fast, sustainable and balanced development across the provinces. The bank would be mandated to further the integration of the economies of the provinces and the balanced development of the country. The bank would have its head office in the capital and over time would have an implementation agency in every province across the country. The head office and the provincial agencies would have a strong project design and implementation capability.

The size of the Democratic Republic of the Congo, the level of developmental challenges, the diversity of the natural resources, and the amount of resources necessary for the balanced and sustainable development of the country all justify this initiative.

The project could be put together very quickly and may prove to be one of the best initiatives to jump-start the economy and put the Congo back on the road to sustainable development. Of course, the project would require a strong political will and enormous resources that can now be mobilized thanks to the favourable outlook generated after the recent general elections. For example, the recent 8.5 billion dollars of Chinese credit to the Democratic Republic of the Congo could be channelled through this bank and make it a strong local implementation agency. Assistance could be obtained from the China Development Bank or other experienced bilateral development institutions in establishing the International Bank for the Reconstruction and Development of the Congo.

While setting up such an institution, it is important to ensure that the last word belongs to the Congo; any other donor (country or institution) would only be a complementary to the country's own efforts. The control over the decision-making process is key, but a strong governance structure would be in place to ensure transparent and efficient use of resources. For example, such an institution can initiate financing of major projects such as railroads, airports, ports, housing for all, mining development, SMEs, microfinance, infrastructures, private sector operations, roads, support to key public enterprises, start-ups, etc. These kinds of projects are not easily initiated by the current local and international financial infrastructures, but with a lead from the country's own development bank, both the local and international financial communities would have no choice but to follow the institution in its catalytic role. The management of the institution and the governance structure in place would be such that the bank would be able to raise money in the long run through local and international bonds issuance and other financial market instruments. Such a bank would give to the country a true development tool under its control that it can effectively use to achieve specific development goals. The IBRDC could be also structured to have a strong policy advice capability so as to have a reasonable input into the design and implementation of the provincial and national development strategies. The bank would build up the necessary knowledge and expertise on development issues in the DRC, to become the entry point for anyone interested in them.

The bank would raise its financing from subscribed and paid-in capital, debt issuance and financial commitments and pledges from Tier I and Tier II shareholders and from donors. The replenishment sessions would be organized every three to five years to raise financial commitments from shareholders and donors. These commitments would serve to support the level of activities during the following three to five years and would be the basis for preparing the institution's work programme for the period.

If a structured and soundly researched implementation study is carried out rapidly, the bank could be established and operational within twelve months. The study could include the drafting of the IBRDC's bylaws or statutes, as well as operational manuals along with the details of the implementation arrangements and the financing plan.

Establishing the IBRDC could be one of the strongest signs to the Congolese community and also to the international community that the Democratic Republic of the Congo has effectively started to work towards its reconstruction following the recent general elections. The timing is right for such a decision as an elected government and institutions are already in place and all eyes are now turned to their signals and policy actions in the aftermath of the recent multiparty elections.

The Congolese Industrial Development Bank

The Congolese Industrial Development Bank (CIDB) would be established as a step to provide credit and other facilities to industries, particularly medium and large-scale enterprises. The CIDB would source funds from commercial banks, the BCC, the central government and some bilateral donors.

The Congolese Bank for Commerce and Industry

The government would establish the Congo Bank for Commerce and Industry (CBCI) in the wake of its indigenization of the economy policy. The CBCI would be set up to develop national enterprise on a small and medium scale. Sources of funds for CBCI would be subsidies from the government and the BCC, through penalties imposed on commercial and merchant banks for credit short-falls on loans to small and medium-scale enterprises. The bank would also engage in shares underwriting, project identification and feasibility studies.

The Congolese Agricultural and Cooperative Bank

The Congolese Agricultural and Cooperative Bank (CACB) should be established mainly to finance agricultural development projects and allied industries. In its operations, the bank would usually interact with central and provincial ministries of agriculture. It would also source its funds from government subsidies, credit short-falls on agricultural loans by commercial and merchant banks through the BCC, and loans from international financial institutions such as the African Development Bank (ADB), the European Investment Bank (EIB) and the International Fund for Agricultural Development (IFAD).

The Urban Development Bank

Congolese cities experience problems of inadequate housing, transportation, electricity and water supply. In order to create a greater capacity for dealing with these problems, the government should establish the Urban Development Bank (UDB) with an initial authorized capital of $250 million, of which $100 million would be subscribed by the three tiers of government (central, state and local). The bank would be operated strictly as an independent profit-making institution and would provide financial resources to both the public and private sectors for the development of urban dwelling, mass transportation and public utilities. The UDB might, with the approval of the minister of finance, raise funds in a foreign currency. Like other specialized banks, the UDB would be exempted from some of the provisions of the Banks and Other Financial Institutions Law of 2002.

Other financial institutions and funds

There are or might be other institutions and funds within the financial system that play important intermediating roles. The institutions might include: insurance companies, finance companies, bureaux de change, primary mortgage institutions, the Industrial Promotion Fund, the Congolese Social Insurance Trust Fund, and the National Social Security Institute.

Insurance companies

The monopoly currently given to the Société Nationale d'Assurance (SONAS) would be broken up as the sector is liberalized. A National Insurance Commission would be established to replace the Insurance Division of the Ministry of Finance as the regulatory organ in the industry. The insurance companies to be developed would consist of life and non-life as well as those which engage in both activities, and reinsurance firms. They would mobilize relatively long-term funds and act as financial intermediaries. Their investments would mainly be in government securities and the mortgage industry. The Congolese insurance industry is expected to grow tremendously over the years.

A Congo Reinsurance Corporation should be established to provide insurance cover for insurance companies. In addition, the Corporation should assist the government in achieving its economic and social objectives in the field of insurance and reinsurance. All registered insurance companies in the Congo would be required to reinsure at least 20 per cent of premiums collected by the Congo Reinsurance Corporation.

Finance companies

Finance companies are institutions that specialize in short-term non-bank financial intermediation. They mobilize funds from the investing public in the form of borrowing and provide, among others, facilities for local purchase orders (LPOs) and project financing, equipment leasing, debt factoring and venture capital companies. The government and Parliament would be compelled to adopt a law to bring finance companies under the direct control and supervision of the BCC.

Bureaux de change

In order to broaden the foreign exchange market and improve access to foreign exchange, especially for small users, bureaux de change have been authorized since 1998. Several bureaux de change have been licensed and are supervised by the BCC.

Primary mortgage institutions

Primary mortgage institutions (PMIs) should operate within the framework of a law to be enacted by Parliament. Essentially, PMIs would mobilize savings for the development of the housing sector. In reaction to distress in the sector, the National Mortgage Bank of the Congo would apply tight surveillance of the institutions by issuing a 'clean bill of health' to selected mortgage institutions. The share capital requirement for new primary mortgage institutions would be set at $10 million. Incentives should be provided to the first ten mortgage banks to be registered within the next five years.

The Industrial Promotion Fund

The Industrial Promotion Fund (IPF) was set up as a funding mechanism aimed at bridging the gap in the provision of local or foreign funds to small and medium-sized enterprises. Going forward, the resources of the IPF are to be mainly contributions from the government, the BCC and foreign sources from foreign governments and the African Development Bank. Prospective beneficiary enterprises should be 100 per cent Congo-owned.

The Congolese Social Insurance Trust Fund

The Congolese Social Insurance Trust Fund (CSITF) would be established with the main objective to adopt a more comprehensive social security scheme for Congolese private sector employees. The scheme would differ from the National Social Security Institute (INSS) which would provide the same benefits for civil servants. Congolese private sector employees would be required to contribute 2.5 per cent, while their employees would be required to contribute 5 per cent of the gross monthly emolument to the CSITF. Workers in enterprises employing more than 25 persons are to be automatically registered by their employers.

The National Social Security Institute

The National Social Security Institute (INSS) would be restructured to be financially viable and transparent in its management and accounts. It would continue to have the objective of providing comprehensive social security schemes for Congolese public sector employees.

Conclusion

This chapter constitutes a vision in the form of an action plan to restructure not only the Central Bank, but also to redesign the other components of the financial sector in the Democratic Republic of the Congo.

The plan can be implemented over a ten-year period and should result in a strong currency and a diversified and well-functioning financial system. This vision is designed to be a comprehensive long-term reform agenda for the financial system and represents an articulated Financial Sector Strategy for the Democratic Republic of the Congo.

6
A Strategic Agenda for the Currency

The preceding chapter has laid down the agenda designed to restructure, refocus and strengthen the Democratic Republic of the Congo's financial system. This chapter is devoted to an important part of our 'vision for a strong currency'. The chapter provides additional elements of the reform agenda designed to position the Congolese franc to become a credible currency. In this light, the agenda would be complemented by reforms designed to stabilize the exchange rate, reduce inflation, restructure the overall denominations of the national currency and introduce coins, as well as to promote the efficiency of the payments system.

All these reforms would be driven by medium- and long-term objectives to ensure economic prosperity for the Democratic Republic of the Congo, and for the Democratic Republic of the Congo to become one of Africa's major financial centres by the year 2025. Only a sustained stable macroeconomic environment and a sound and vibrant financial system can propel the economy to achieve our national desire to become one of the fifty largest economies in the world within the next thirty years. The 'Strategic Agenda for the Congolese Franc' should therefore be launched as the first phase of this broad reform agenda.

According to the Central Bank of the Democratic Republic of the Congo Law no. 005/2002 of 7 May 2002, the key objectives of the Central Bank would be to: (i) ensure monetary and price stability; (ii) issue legal tender currency in the Democratic Republic of the Congo; (iii) maintain external reserves to safeguard the international value of the legal tender currency; (iv) promote a sound financial system in the Democratic Republic of the Congo; and (v) act as banker for, and provide economic and financial advice to the central government.

During this phase, the Central Bank would focus on the Congolese franc, which means that the Bank intends to give greater emphasis to the most important function of central banks everywhere in the world, namely, to issue legal tender currency and to defend its value (domestically by ensuring low inflation, and externally by ensuring an appropriate and stable exchange rate regime). The specific objective of phase one of the reforms is to make the Congolese franc the currency of reference in Africa, and thus a strategic catalyst for achieving the goal of an international financial centre as well as promoting the Democratic Republic of the Congo's rapid economic development.

Reforms agenda and expected outcomes

During phase one of the programme, most of the reforms would focus on structural and institutional aspects, and would include the following: (1) strengthening the institutional framework for the conduct of monetary policy; (2) recapitalization and consolidation of the banking sector, including the recapitalization of the Central Bank, and recapitalization and consolidation of commercial banks; (3) a programme to rationalize government ownership of any commercial bank (to a clearly stated limit to be approved by the government); (4) improving transparency and corporate governance; (5) adoption of a policy of zero tolerance of misreporting and data misreporting, and strict adherence to the anti-money laundering regulations; (6) implementing the Basel II principles and risk-based supervision; (7) reforming the payments system for efficiency – especially the electronic payments system; (8) reforming the exchange rate management system – and increased liberalization of the foreign exchange market; (9) restructuring the Hôtel de Monnaies along more efficient lines; (10) addressing issues of technology and skills in the banking industry, especially in risk management; (11) broadening the scope of the microfinance policy and regulatory framework to serve the as yet unmet banking needs of 95 per cent of the public; (12) reforming the pensions sector, the consumer credit industry and the mortgage system; (13) forging strategic alliances and partnerships between Congolese banks and foreign financial institutions, especially in the area of reserve and asset management; (14) establishing the Congo Finance Corporation (CFC) as the first private sector Congolese investment bank; (15) motivating Congolese banks to develop nationwide and globally; (16) creation of the Congolese Stock Exchange; (17) upgrading the banking supervision to be risk-based, consolidated and more rigorous; (18) reforming the mortgage, SME, and consumer credit sectors; and (19) enactment and enforcement of the dud cheque offences policies to be approved by Parliament.

The strategic agenda

The thrust of the agenda focuses on the Congolese franc as the national currency of the Democratic Republic of the Congo – to realign its denominations and ensure its stability and global integration. These measures would help to deepen the reforms of the financial system and national economy, and make the franc the currency of reference in Africa, thereby facilitating our quest for international financial status.

The new focus is an extension of the previously proposed currency redesign and re-issuance of the lower denominations and the introduction of coins. The goals would be to redesign the currency after ten years (contrary to the international norm of currency redesign after six to eight years), drive down the cost of currency printing and combat dollarization. In the light of the new mandate of the BCC Law of 7 May 2002 to 'ensure monetary and price stability', as well as the vision for a strong currency, it is imperative for us to evolve a more comprehensive strategy for the Democratic Republic of the Congo to have a reference currency.

Currency redenomination and liberalization are not without risks, especially for small open economies such as the Democratic Republic of the Congo. However, the time is auspicious for such reforms especially in the light of the following enabling conditions: (1) the overall commitment of the newly elected central government to sustaining macroeconomic and other structural reforms; (2) the advent of the third Republic and the establishment of key democratic institutions; (3) the growing banking system powering a new economy and capital market; (4) inflation expected to be down to a low double digit figure; (5) positive GDP growth of about 5 per cent and above; (6) relative exchange rate stability within the last ten months; (6) positive capital inflows; (7) upcoming debt relief under the Highly Indebted Poor Countries Initiative; (8) strong growth of mining exports; and (9) promulgation of the Central Bank Law not permitting the BCC to grant ways and means advances to the government exceeding 10 per cent of the previous year's revenue and ensuring that such financing is retired before the end of the financial year. (Indeed, the BCC should not be positively disposed to granting any ways and means advances to the government if its own financial condition continues to be strained.)

It is in view of the foregoing enabling conditions, and the vision for a strong currency of reference in Africa, that the Board of Directors of the Central Bank of the Congo, the National Assembly, the Senate and the government would be asked to approve the following comprehensive agenda for the franc.

Another currency reform

A person arriving for the first time in the Democratic Republic of the Congo may not realize that he or she has actually reached it. From the airport to the city centre, the American dollar is widely used. Few people want to use the Congolese franc for various reasons, some of which are the high inflation that has eroded confidence in the currency, the poor condition of bank notes and the sheer volume of local currency necessary to conduct even a small transaction.

Beyond the personal attachment to a legal tender that has become worthless, the country needs to restructure the entire currency structure and introduce new notes and coins to be managed differently than in the past. The new currency might be obtained by dividing the existing bank notes by 565,[1] and issuing new bank notes and coins. This would entail a total currency exchange and phasing-out of all the existing denominations within the next two years. Effectively, at the current exchange rate, this policy would mean that the franc versus US dollar exchange rate would then be around F1.0 to US$1. All franc assets, prices and contracts would be redenominated by dividing the existing value by the same coefficient of 565 with effect from this date. Effectively, this plan would restore the value of the franc (in the short term) close to what it was in 1998 when the franc was first launched.

Redenomination and reintroduction of a totally new currency structure (notes and coins), following the progress so far with other reforms and the enabling conditions in the economy today, are designed to do the following: better anchor inflationary expectations, strengthen public confidence in the franc, make for easier conversion to other currencies, reverse the tendency for currency substitution, eliminate higher denomination notes with lower value ones, reduce the cost of production, distribution and processing of currency, promote the usage of coins and thus a more efficient pricing and payments system, and lay the foundation for the convertibility of the franc as well as make it the 'reference currency' in Africa. This improved Congolese profile would allow the country to play an important role when the African Union-sponsored common currency in Africa materializes. The Congo must therefore lead the way in terms of a properly aligned currency structure and sound monetary policy framework so as to play a key role at the African level.

Several countries in the world have undertaken currency redenomination at various times and for different reasons, including: Afghanistan (2002); Angola (1995, 1999); Argentina (1970, 1983, 1985, 1992); Bolivia (1963, 1987); Brazil (1967, 1970, 1986, 1989, 1990, 1993, 1994); China

(1955); Germany (1923, 1948); Ghana (2007); Israel (1948, 1960, 1980, 1985); Mexico (1993, 1996); South Korea (1962); and Turkey (2005). Evidently, many countries, like the Democratic Republic of the Congo, have had to undertake redenomination more than once. In the case of Brazil, it had to do it many times before it got it right. The major challenge is to undertake other complementary reforms, particularly macroeconomic reforms that would underpin price stability and continuing confidence in the economy. This is where I believe that the Democratic Republic of the Congo's experience is likely to be different from others', having learned from the experiences of other countries and from its own experience over the last fifty years.

Consequently, as necessary complements to the currency redenomination, additional measures should be introduced: (1) adoption of an inflation-targeting framework for the conduct of monetary policy; (2) progressive and gradual current account liberalization and convertibility; (3) strengthening of the legal and regulatory framework for business; and (4) pursuit of an aggressive policy to attract foreign investment.

Framework for the conduct of monetary policy

In the light of the new mandate as contained in the new Central Bank Act urging the BCC to 'ensure monetary and price stability' as well as the need to provide a transparent, credible framework to lock in inflationary expectations, the BCC should adopt an inflation target as the nominal anchor for monetary policy. A low and stable inflation rate should be the Central Bank's primary long-term goal. Focusing on inflation targeting does not mean that the BCC would not be interested in other broader objectives of macroeconomic policy – output growth, employment, exchange rate and balance of payments. Rather, an inflation-targeting framework would enable the BCC to pursue these objectives in a more disciplined and consistent manner rather than through the ad hoc processes of the past. Locking in inflationary expectations is one effective way of ensuring that the currency redenomination would be sustainable. The outcome of this new framework would greatly improve the credibility of the BCC as the monetary authority, as well as deepen the financial markets and promote rapid development of a private sector-led economy.

The Central Bank should use the first two years to fully prepare for the introduction of this framework especially in light of the deep technical issues involved. The BCC would collaborate with the National Institute of Statistics in significantly improving the availability of regular and reliable data, especially those of the GDP and more robust measures of the price indices.

Current account liberalization and convertibility

As a necessary complement to the foregoing policy initiatives, and to further deepen the integration of the Congolese financial system and economy into the global economy, the country would have to embark upon progressive and gradual current account liberalization and convertibility within three years. This would entail that the Democratic Republic of the Congo eliminates some restrictions on current account transactions, and move progressively towards full currency convertibility.

Conclusion

These measures constitute a key component of the financial sector strategic agenda in the Democratic Republic of the Congo's quest to become an international financial centre and a major African financial centre. The conditions are now right, and despite the challenges, the country must be determined to ensure effective financial sector reforms design and implementation.

Furthermore, the Democratic Republic of the Congo should be working towards greater transparency in the formulation and implementation of its monetary policy. A new Monetary Policy Committee (MPC) would be constituted urgently in accordance with the new BCC Act, and the minutes of the MPC would be made public. The Central Bank of the Congo must also undertake greater public education about what it does and the reasons for its actions.

It therefore goes without saying that if the franc is properly aligned and can become the 'reference currency', then the goal of a monetary union becomes all the more credible and realizable. The Democratic Republic of the Congo has met some of the primary convergence criteria and hopes to continue working towards these broad goals on a sustained basis. In the meantime, the Democratic Republic of the Congo must continue to make progress in the management of the Central Bank of the Congo and the Congolese franc.

7
Leadership in Managing Changes in Central Banks

Transforming an inefficient central bank into a credible institution entails important changes over a long period of time. When change is necessary, the most important determinant of 'getting through the swamp' is the ability of leadership to lead. The literature on the subject indicates that the nature of the change is secondary to the perceptions that central bank employees have regarding the ability, competence and credibility of senior and middle management to achieve the desired outcome.

Many central banks profess to consider their employees as their most important asset, but all too often their policies, procedures and managerial practices contradict this view. Such contradictions and outdated management practices inhibit improvements in productivity, sap motivation and reduce the performance towards the overall objectives of central banks in emerging economies. Managerial practices must keep pace with the changing workforce in central banks. The workforce of today is better educated and its value systems, career expectations and basic work habits are drastically different from those of the previous generation. Unfortunately many managers of central banks in emerging economies have not changed their style to meet their needs.

Continued adherence to management techniques that may have been acceptable in the past is a serious impediment to any central bank's ability to succeed in today's environment. Employees are looking for more responsibility and more involvement in decisions – particularly those which directly affect them. The traditional authoritarian boss–subordinate relationship is not accepted by the majority of employees today. Staff resistance to outdated management results in minimal performance levels and causes central banks to forfeit required improvements in productivity and efficiency.

A different focus on the relationship of the central bank manager to those being managed can be done without 'giving away the store' and compromising the manager's role of giving direction. For central banks to be successful and credible, it is essential that they update their approach to managing their most important asset: their people.

Many central bank managers are familiar with, and are part of, the evolution of personnel management where new ideas in this field are seized upon as a solution to an existing problem or existing practices are modified and given new impetus. As a consequence, many facets of personnel management in central banks need to be introduced as individual programmes. This often results in a disjointed set of policies and procedures, which are not focused on contributing to institutional goals and often have the opposite effect.

Effective leadership is a quality that central banks need in order to thrive. Responding to change in a central bank is a key function of leadership. Leadership exists at different levels within a central bank. The way each level copes with change and directs the transformation determines how the whole organization changes and how it sustains the new outlook.

Before and during implementation of a change programme in a central bank, it is important to organize information seminars regrouping participants from different departments at all levels: directors, division chiefs, supervisors, high level and support staff. This rich diversity of experience, enhanced by presentations of central bank case examples, must form the backdrop to a lively discussion on the role played by leadership and organizational culture in transformation processes. These exercises help central bank staff to buy into the change programme, a necessary precondition for its success.

Importance of implementing changes in a central bank

Change in central banks covers a vast field of activities, generally aimed at improving performance, productivity and efficiency. This can be achieved in different ways – through growth, innovation and skills development; downsizing, layoffs and replacements; shifts in activities or resources; or a combination of these. However, the way in which a central bank is transformed, and the way in which that transformation is managed, depends almost exclusively on the style of leadership and the culture of the central bank.

It is important to keep in mind that implementing changes is what makes and breaks a good leader in a central bank. Ideas first put forward by Aristotle and Plato in 300 BC still have credence in the twenty-first century. However, global relocation, outsourcing, as well as the drive for constant innovation, create new challenges for leadership. New approaches to work and efficiency can overturn traditional ideas and raise questions such as: What sort of leadership is appropriate in a central bank at a specific stage? Where does power in a central bank lie? Is it shifting from those with charisma to those with knowledge? Would an increase of women in leadership roles challenge a predominantly masculine view of leadership, and therefore produce a different style of leadership? What kind of culture in a central bank would support and enhance good leadership? And how can good leadership and an appropriate culture help achieve the successful transformation of a central bank from a dormant to a dynamic and efficient institution?

Setting the stage for changes in a central bank

In today's central bank environment, leaders face significant challenges: (i) business is more complex, customized and competitive; (ii) the 'war for talent' means that people are more important than strategies; (iii) the dwindling supply of highly qualified executives is accompanied by greater job mobility among this group; (iv) the rise of the knowledge economy and reliance on technology; and (v) the potential pitfalls of dispersed and virtual working teams.

A changing central bank may put together case studies that offer very different angles on these issues. For each of these issues, participants in central bank change seminars must be invited to look at context, culture and change and to consider the following questions: (1) Considering the size of the central bank, what are the drivers of change? (2) What type of central bank is it? Networked? Hierarchical? Where does the power lie? (3) What is the organization's leadership style? How and where is it exercised? Are different parts of the central bank characterized differently? (4) What is the leadership structure? How are decisions reached? Is this appropriate for the central bank's mission, role and purpose? (5) How has the central bank's culture changed to meet the shifting environment? How does it plan to change? (6) What do participants know about the central bank's people? What is the approach to employees?

Characteristics of an effective leadership

The word 'leadership' means one who sets directions. It is important to highlight the characteristics of a leader in a central bank. It is a known fact that leaders always take advantage of key opportunities for change, but they may do so with different styles. A leader can be: (i) a charismatic, godlike figure representing power and control; (ii) a hero or heroine: a visionary leader who inspires trust and loyalty; (iii) a 'fixer' who makes everything all right; (iv) a steersman or woman who sets directions; (v) a coach and mentor functioning as facilitator; (vi) a good mother or father who acts as a caring and competent manager of the company, taking care of all aspects of the company including emotional and organizational issues.

It is generally agreed that leadership, and styles of leadership, play a critical role in driving change in a central bank, that there are different sources of leadership and that the definition of leadership varies from situation to situation.

Effective leadership is a key to success for a central bank

Over the years, I have learned that leadership is a key factor affecting a central bank's credibility and efficiency. Leadership can be broken down into three broad categories: institutional vision, setting an example and expectations.

Institutional vision

A manager in a central bank is a leader. As such, central bank employees view the leader or manager (consciously or not) as the role model for success. Employees emulate his or her belief system and attitudes towards work, clients, central bank staff and the external environment. If success and performance are important to the leader, they will inevitably be important to their staff.

To be a good leader, one needs a goal and a vision for the central bank. The first step to creating this vision is through an institutional mission statement. A good institutional mission statement includes two components: the message and the truth. The message clearly states the attitude, values and mission of the central bank mandate to everyone, including the employees. It should be clear, short and simple. It is like a telephone number – if it is too long or complicated, no one will remember it. Regardless of the message presented in the mission statement, it must be one that central bank management honestly believes in and is totally committed to. Otherwise, the employees will reject the statement as mere window dressing, and the central bank's level of performance will surely suffer. The institutional mission statement should be professionally printed, framed and openly displayed so that everyone has the chance to see the new vision and to understand its purpose.

Setting an example

As the de facto leader, the central bank manager often forgets the impact that his or her actions have upon the troops. As the role model, the manager must be on his toes and prepared to lead by example. This means that the manager must be involved and visible by being a day-to-day presence, touring the facility, meeting with employees and asking them about their problems, thereby demonstrating an interest in the people. This is a prerequisite for leadership – if the manager's staff believe that he or she has their well-being at heart, they are more likely to follow their lead.

Stay down to earth: employees do not expect (and probably do not want) the central bank governor or president to do menial tasks like cleaning up the rubbish in the parking lot, but getting one's hands a little dirty shows the employees that he or she is not above any job that helps the central bank meet its mission, and it builds employee loyalty and respect.

Practice what you preach about performance and work ethics: as the ultimate decision-maker, the central bank manager has to remind his or her employees constantly that the public is the actor who really delivers the pay cheques. Optimizing public service and keeping the public satisfied means that the central bank places the public first, and the central bank management is willing to allocate the resources that allows its staff to provide excellent service and deliver high performance.

Share the wealth (but don't flaunt it): when the central bank succeeds and times are good, its employees should share in the success. Employees should receive recognition for good performance or good years, but even in bad years, they should receive a small bonus. The manager should also be discrete and avoid displays of overt materialism while helping the staff to feel that they're moving up in the world.

Share the credit: although central bank management may be the main reason for success in the area of mandated objectives, central bank management will get more mileage by sharing the credit with the staff. Everyone appreciates praise and recognition, and sharing the credit (or giving all the credit to the staff) is one of the keys to employee job satisfaction, helping management to build a better team that will excel in its future endeavours. A your-success-is-my-success attitude goes a long way towards ensuring that everyone in the central bank succeeds.

Expectations

As leaders, most of us assume that our managers – through central bank-wide osmosis – know exactly what is expected of them. Unfortunately, that is usually far from the truth. The subordinates want the leader to establish written goals and objectives. They want a system in place to measure themselves as well as to be measured by their leader. The best way to let the employees know what is expected of them is through a management by objective (MBO) programme. Under an MBO programme, a set of written objectives is developed jointly between each key employee and his or her respective leader at the end of the fiscal year. These are the goals for the next year. To get the most from the employees, goals should be high yet obtainable. If they are unreasonable, then they become worthless as a management tool. Reviews should be carried out monthly (verbal) and quarterly (written). Putting everything in writing makes it a commitment and makes the difference.

The list of what constitutes good leadership is endless, but the bottom line on leadership is straightforward: the leader must practise what he or she preaches, and project a positive attitude towards both public and employees. He or she is the role model for institutional behaviour. The leader must set the example; no one else can.

Central bank leaders play a critical role during change implementation, the period from the announcement of change through the installation of the change. During this middle period, the central bank organization may become unstable, characterized by confusion, fear, loss of direction, reduced productivity, and lack of clarity about direction and mandate. It can be an emotional period, with central bank employees grieving for what is lost, and initially unable to look to the future.

During this period, effective central bank leaders need to focus on two things. First, the feelings and confusion of employees must be acknowledged and validated. Second, the central bank leader must work with employees to begin creating a new vision of the altered workplace, and help employees to understand the direction of the future. Focusing only on feelings, however, may result in wallowing. That is why it is necessary to initiate the central bank's movement into the new ways of working. But focusing only on the new vision may result in the perception that the central bank leader is out of touch, cold and uncaring. A key part of central bank leadership in this phase is knowing when to focus on the pain, and when to focus on building and moving into the future.

In my professional career, I have observed closely the US Federal Reserve Bank under the leadership of three different leaders over the last three decades. Paul Volcker, Alan Greenspan and Ben Bernanke were chairmen of the US Federal Reserve at different times. Each of them had a different leadership style that had a tremendous and profound impact on the central bank and the financial market. Paul Volcker is credited with instilling in the central bank staff a sense of independence and an anti-inflation posture. His words were followed and watched closely by the financial market and proved to be highly accurate. Alan Greenspan brought to monetary policy a degree of transparency that never existed before, and equalled Paul Volcker in his credibility with the financial market, although his close relationship with President Bill Clinton and Treasury Secretary Robert Rubin blurred the notion of central bank independence from the executive branch of the government. Nevertheless, he was viewed as a successful leader whose decisive actions in monetary policy committees matched his words, language and style.

Since assuming the chairmanship of the Fed, Ben Bernanke[1] is struggling to make his leadership's consensus-building style credible and effective in monetary policy discussions. While Alan Greenspan left no doubt during FOMC meetings that he was the one calling the shots, Ben Bernanke is viewed as being too democratic a leader at a time when strong and decisive leadership is needed at the Fed. Charles Plosser, the President of the Philadelphia Fed who is one of Bernanke's Open Market Committee colleagues, admits that he worries about the extent to which 'democracy', however admirable, has dulled the Fed's aura and, perhaps, its ability to lead.[2] Paul Volcker declared in his assessment of the central bank under Ben Bernanke that 'the Fed is not really in control of the situation'.[3]

The above illustrates the fact that any central bank needs an effective and decisive leadership to be successful. Lack of such leadership can mean, as the declining stock market reactions have shown following each announcement or public appearance by Ben Bernanke, that there is an urgent need for change in the leadership, the leadership style or the central bank itself within the purview of the law and the central bank act. Without such a deliberate and fundamental change, success may become a distant dream at the Fed under Chairman Ben Bernanke.

Balancing the internal and external environment

Leaders do not exist in isolation and neither do their central banks. Leaders who are as in touch with the external environment in which their central bank operates, as with its internal environment, and who can adapt their direction to changing circumstances are more likely to continue as leaders of successful central banks.

How leaders achieve successful changes in central banks

I would like to call the readers' attention to two main dimensions of leadership in central banks: (i) concern for the task and (ii) concern for the people you are relying on to achieve the task.

Central bank leaders achieve successful change by constantly balancing these two dimensions. In this context, 'successful' means not only reaching objectives, but also staying with and sustaining the change until such time as other objectives take their place. The presence of clear central bank values provides a touchstone when the company and its workforce are engaged in a change process. How these values are described, and the degree to which they express concern for the task or concern for people, varies from one central bank to another.

Just as the work environment can affect the style of leadership, so too can the stage through which the central bank is moving. Successful leaders of change in central banks may not always be successful leaders of stability, consolidation and continuity, or thriving leaders in periods of massive disruption. These different conditions require a different style of leadership, which may not necessarily be found in the existing senior management of central banks. There are different ways for leaders to achieve successful change in central banks, which include: (i) taking risks; (ii) recognizing the politics involved; (iii) paying attention to detail; (iv) staying close to the heart; (v) creating an impression; (vi) creating awareness of the crisis; (vii) building a new identity; (viii) demonstrating the need for change; (ix) communicating in a clear and timely manner; (x) developing a vision, charting the roadmap and winning everybody's commitment to it; (xi) establishing common shared goals; (xii) being visible, credible and responsible as a leader of change; and (xiii) being clear about sanctions and rewards, both collective and individual.

Developing and sustaining a culture of change

Changes in central banks are uncomfortable because, in general, people want the status quo to remain. They become even more uncomfortable when managers isolate themselves and do not have the answers to questions from the central bank staff. Indeed, it is better not to communicate than to misinform. However, not to communicate at all creates a climate of fear and mistrust around change. A culture of change in a central bank must be built on intelligent communication and emotional intelligence which results in appropriate disclosure, avoiding the temptation to hide uncertainty with buzzwords and clichés.

There is a distinction to be made between leaders of change, generally present in senior and top management, and change agents, who can be found anywhere in the central bank. A good leader in a central bank nurtures change agents through training and development, listening and, sometimes, remuneration.

Sustaining a culture of change in a central bank requires continuous effort and investment. There is a world of difference between a sustainable culture of change within a central bank and perpetual reorganizations. Nurturing and sustaining change may require attributes and styles which may not be familiar to the male-dominated world of central bank leaders. The good leader, if she or he does not already possess them, needs to find these attributes and styles within the central bank and support them.

The unfolding economic meltdown in the United States that began in 2007 with the subprime mortgage credit crunch should call for a great deal of sympathy for central banks around the world with the challenges that they face to implement changes and maintain price stability. Once praised for facilitating high growth and low inflation, central banks now find themselves in a delicate and conflicting situation: should they risk fuelling future inflation in order to avoid a recession induced by a market-driven credit crunch, or maintain low inflationary expectations at the risk of both depressed economic growth and serious financial market dislocations? Too many observers have cited changes in personnel as an important part of the explanation for this shift. Tempting as this is, it is not appropriate. The better approach is to analyse how far global financial transformations have eroded the potency of traditional central bank tools. Central bankers now operate in a world where monetary policy influences only a small part of the fluctuations in overall liquidity in the economy. The extent to which the market itself expands and contracts liquidity, has taken over as the main driver. As a result, successive interest rate increases did little to contain excesses during the expansion in market liquidity that ended in the summer of 2007. Interest rate cuts are having difficulty countering the forces of endogenous liquidity contraction that are being accentuated by the impact of the large losses at many financial institutions.

This transformation is challenging for central banks, especially in a world that has seen them as the wise guardians of responsible macroeconomic policies. The challenge is particularly serious for the US Federal Reserve, with a dual mandate: controlling inflation and maintaining solid economic growth and employment.

In response, some central bankers have shifted to a more responsive and opportunistic approach. Indeed, this was a big factor in the decision by the *Financial Times* to name Jean-Claude Trichet, President of the European Central Bank, as its 'person of the year' for 2007. Not all central bankers have his ability, leadership and willingness to respond in a bold and timely fashion to a serious crisis. Therefore they need to rely on structural adaptations to address the difficulties. To this end, five items should be pursued. First, they need to improve their understanding of the new financial landscape. This is an absolute must when it comes to the activities of the big investment banks, especially those with privileged access to various central bank financing windows. It would help counter some of the systemic risk posed by off-balance-sheet conduits, lax risk management practices and aggressive financial alchemy.

Second, central bankers need to revisit the conventional wisdom that calls for separation of monetary policy and bank supervision. With the growing impact of endogenous liquidity such separation can inhibit rather than facilitate the conduct of good monetary policy – as recently discovered by the Bank of England.

Third, they need to improve, directly or indirectly, scrutiny of financial activities that have migrated outside their formal jurisdiction. At the minimum, this involves better coordination with and skill transfers to supervisory bodies in the insurance, mortgage and pensions domains.

Fourth, excessive reliance on interest rate changes as the tool of monetary policy should give way to a broader approach. This entails greater recourse to open market operations and further revamps to the discount window in the US in particular.

Finally, central bankers need to work harder to manage policy expectations and improve communication. The public should have clarity about their policy goals and operating processes, but also be aware of what central banks cannot do. This is important when the onus of a suitable policy response to the subprime debacle should be placed, either directly or indirectly, at the feet of the fiscal agencies.

Central banks must urgently act on these five items. If they do not, the damage will go well beyond eroding any chance they still have to reclaim a leadership role on liquidity management, albeit a more modest one. Instead, they will be condemned to walk behind the financial market parade. In the process, they will continue to be blamed for, and expected to clean up, the occasional large mess, but with declining effectiveness.

Conclusion

Because a number of central banks in emerging economies are eager to embark on a comprehensive agenda for change with a view to becoming more credible, it is important to keep in mind the necessary flexibility and intelligence to manage the change process so as to make it a positive experience for those involved.

Changes must be clearly communicated and carefully implemented by both central bank management and staff and must have strong political support. Nobody can be left behind if the result is to be successful. In sum, the value of a central bank is its people, policies, systems and infrastructures.

Keeping people informed, up to date and motivated under a strong leadership is the best way to ensure that positive changes are implemented effectively. After all, strong and visionary leadership and good people are the lifeblood for the transformation of ineffective institutions into credible central banks. As a change leader, the central bank top management needs to establish credibility and a track record of effective decision-making, so that there is trust in its ability to figure out what is necessary to bring the organization through successfully.

Playing a leadership role in a central bank is not easy. Not only does an effective central bank leader have a responsibility to lead, but as an employee himself, he has to deal with his own reactions to the change, and his role in it. If one is ineffective in leading change, the leader will bear a very heavy personal load. Since the leader is accountable for the performance of the central bank, he or she will have to deal with the ongoing loss of productivity and criticism that can result from poorly managed change, not to mention the potential impact on his or her own enjoyment of the job of leadership.

Conclusion

Of key importance to the effective operation of the Central Bank of the Congo within the government are: a well-designed policy mandate; a high degree of formal instrument independence; complementary informal relationships to ensure appropriate coordination without undermining instrument independence; a disciplined, regular process of legislative oversight; and a high degree of transparency and disclosure. The result would be a good trade-off among government-mandated objectives, instrument independence, flexibility, and accountability. But this very same trade-off may leave open opportunities for political interference and continuing energy and focus will be required – both inside the Central Bank of the Congo and within the rest of government – to sustain the operational autonomy and independence of the central bank.

As a result, we should not regard the operational autonomy or independence of the Central Bank of the Congo as unassailable but rather as a principle that has to be defended now that the country has an elected political leadership operating within stable and democratic institutions. With this new order, the days of hyperinflation will be over, and the Congolese currency can be expected to be stable and strong in the years to come, provided that the government maintains a strict budgetary discipline and creates an environment conducive to increased private sector investments. If these reforms are undertaken, the Central Bank of the Congo, just like many other central banks around the world, will find itself unusually strong and influential. I refrain from saying popular, a word that is not easily associated with institutions which often have to say 'no'.[1]

Although not always popular, it is with a recognition of necessity that in recent years several important countries have rewritten their national laws and even their constitutions in order to provide a high degree of institutional autonomy for their central banks. As a result, many central banks have gained a clearly dominant voice in monetary policy, and often a large influence over general economic policy.

Central banks must work hard every day to earn the trust that the public places in them. Central bankers are not super humans; they cannot be guaranteed to be benevolent or omniscient. They will perform best within an institution that is given a clear objective and that is held accountable by the public. Conversely, the public would be ill advised to put 'blind trust' in central bankers. Price stability, preserving the value of money, is the precondition for a well-functioning market economy, for economic and social stability, and for a free and prosperous society. Price stability is too important for society to be left 'on trust' to the vagaries of the political process or to the whims of individual central bankers. It requires building solid and strong independent institutions which are dedicated to serving and defending the common good of price stability. It is both economically sensible as well as democratically legitimate for society to delegate such a limited and well-defined task to an independent central bank. Such an act of delegation confers an obligation on the central bank to fulfil this trust and to be held accountable. Faith may be required, but control by an attentive public will also be needed. Then there will be good reason to trust independent central banks with the maintenance of price stability.

The Democratic Republic of the Congo is no exception. The promulgation of the Central Bank Law in 2002 with a clear recognition of its independence or institutional autonomy was in itself a milestone. But independence on paper and independence in practice are two different things. It is now time to adopt the process and practices which provide true independence while balancing them with the basic principles of accountability in order to meet the requirements of the emerging democracy in the Democratic Republic of the Congo.

As much as we may welcome greater autonomy for central bank decision-making in the Democratic Republic of the Congo, we have to recognize that an independent central bank is not an end in itself. It certainly cannot substitute for trust in elected officials and effective central and provincial governments. The very idea of emphasizing greater independence in an increasingly interdependent financial world strikes a dissonant note. Behind the slogan of central bank independence or institutional autonomy, we need a clearer understanding of its real significance in today's world and of its limitations as well. Accountability is a way to limit the full and uncontrollable temper of an independent central bank in the Democratic Republic of the Congo and elsewhere.

A credible central bank can effectively lead the process of financial sector reform in a country. There is no doubt that financial sector development can make an important contribution to economic growth and poverty reduction in the Democratic Republic of the Congo and indeed in any emerging democracy. This is particularly true in the Democratic Republic of the Congo, however, whose financial sector is particularly underdeveloped, and without it economic development would be certainly constrained, even if other necessary conditions such as stable institutions, return to peace and stability, and macroeconomic stability and infrastructure development are met. Transforming ineffective institutions into credible central banks requires substantial changes in people, systems, infrastructures, procedures, policies and instruments. Changes must be clearly communicated and carefully implemented by both central bank management and staff and must have strong political support. I know, personally, that the success of a regime of central bank independence in an emerging country depends on the chemistry between the president of the country and the governor of the central bank and, indeed, on the personal skills of the numerous players involved, including the prime minister, the minister of finance and the legislators.

I hope to have laid out a clear vision for the reform of the central bank and the financial sector to make them useful tools for the development of any emerging country. While some might take offence at my advocating a greater role for the government in the financial sector than many so-called conservative economists might wish, I would question the wisdom of the prescriptions of the usual 'hands off' approach advocated by the traditionally conditionalities-driven interventions which, in practice, have never been successful anywhere in the world. I hope that this book will inspire emerging countries around the world to design their own home-grown financial sector policies. Without a home-grown agenda for the financial sector and the overall economy, success in the area of development will continue to be a distant dream for many emerging countries.

Appendix 1

Countries with explicit deposit insurance

Asia

Bangladesh	Bangladesh Bank
Hong Kong	Hong Kong Deposit Protection Board
India	Deposit Insurance and Credit Guarantee Corporation
Indonesia	Indonesia Deposit Insurance Corporation
Japan	Deposit Insurance Corporation of Japan
Kazakhstan	Kazakhstan Deposit Insurance Fund
Korea	Korea Deposit Insurance Corporation
Malaysia	Malaysia Deposit Insurance Corporation
Philippines	Philippines Deposit Insurance Corporation
Singapore	Singapore Deposit Insurance Corporation
Taiwan	Central Deposit Insurance Corporation
Vietnam	Deposit Insurance of Vietnam

Central America, South America and the Caribbean

Argentina	Seguro de Depositos Sociedad Anonima
Bahamas	Deposit Insurance Corporation
Brazil	Fundo Garantidor de Creditos
Colombia	Fondo de Garantias de Instituciones Financieras
El Salvador	Instituto de Garantia de Depositos
Jamaica	Jamaica Deposit Insurance Corporation
Mexico	Instituto para la Proteccion al Ahorro Bancario
Nicaragua	Nicaraguan Deposit Insurance Fund
Peru	Fondo de Seguro de Depositos
Trinidad and Tobago	Deposit Insurance Corporation
Venezuela	Fondo de Garantia de Depositos y Proteccion Bancaria

Europe

Albania	Albanian Deposit Insurance Agency
Bulgaria	Bulgarian Deposit Insurance Fund
Bosnia and Herzegovina	Deposit Insurance Agency of Bosnia and Herzegovina
Czech Republic	Deposit Insurance Fund Czech Republic
France	Fonds de Garantie des Depots
Hungary	National Deposit Insurance Fund of Hungary
Romania	Deposit Guarantee Fund in the Banking System
Russia	Deposit Insurance Agency
Sweden	Swedish Deposit Guarantee Board
Ukraine	The Deposit Insurance Fund

Middle East and Africa

Jordan	Jordan Deposit Insurance Corporation
Kenya	Deposit Protection Fund Board
Lebanon	Institut National de Garantie des Depots
Morocco	Bank Al-Maghrib, Fonds Collectif de Garantie des Depots
Nigeria	Nigeria Deposit Insurance Corporation
Sudan	Bank Deposit Security Fund
Tanzania	Deposit Insurance Board of Tanzania
Turkey	Savings Deposit Insurance Fund
Zimbabwe	Deposit Protection Board

North America

Canada	Authorité des marchés financiers (Quebec)
Canada	Canada Deposit Insurance Corporation
United States	Federal Deposit Insurance Corporation

Countries planning to establish deposit insurance systems

Asia

Mongolia	Bank of Mongolia
Philippines	Bangko Sentral ng Pilipinas
Singapore	Monetary Authority of Singapore
Thailand	Bank of Thailand

Central America, South America and the Caribbean

Barbados

Europe and Africa

Algeria	Bank of Algeria
South Africa	The National Treasury

Appendix 2

A tribute to the Deutsche Bundesbank

As a student of central banking and monetary policy, I had to review the structure and functioning of several central banks across the world. I did this while preparing my doctoral dissertation on central bank independence, accountability and impact on monetary policy. I learned from this experience that some central banks are successful, and others are not. I learned also that of all the successful central banks in the world, the Deutsche Bundesbank was in a class by itself. It has not only inspired the world, but it has influenced the setting up of today's most successful supranational central bank, the European Central Bank. For that reason, I would like to pay a special tribute to the Deutsche Bundesbank for leading the pack and setting an example that many central banks around the world have to follow.

Legacy of stability passed on to the Eurosystem

Keeping citizens' money as stable as possible has always been the mandate of the Deutsche Bundesbank. As the central bank of the Federal Republic of Germany, it has fulfilled this mandate for half a century more consistently and successfully than almost any other monetary institution in the world – a period of almost sixty years if one includes its predecessor, the Bank Deutscher Länder. The reputation of the Deutschmark as a stable currency has lived on in the euro, the single European currency, since 1999.

Having celebrated its 50th anniversary in 2007, the Deutsche Bundesbank is no longer on everyone's lips when the subject of debate is security and vulnerability or the pros and cons of a stable currency. It is no longer the bank whose interest rate policy has to be followed by the other European central banks if they want to avoid a depreciation of their currencies. In 1999 the Bundesbank transferred its autonomous responsibility for monetary policy to the Eurosystem.

The Bundesbank in the Eurosystem

The Bundesbank in the Eurosystem continues to play a major role in safeguarding the value of the currency and the stability of the financial system. The Bundesbank, together with the other central banks of the Eurosystem and the European Central Bank, is responsible for the euro. As a member of the Governing Council of the European Central Bank, the president of the Bundesbank is involved in formulating European monetary policy. The Bundesbank also performs key tasks for the Eurosystem through its implementation of monetary policy decisions in Germany, supplying the economy with cash, providing cashless payment facilities and managing the reserve assets. Under German law, the Bundesbank is also empowered to participate in banking supervision and to advise the federal government on matters of monetary policy importance. Finally, it has a major role in communicating European monetary policy to the German public.

However, the Bundesbank's importance for the Eurosystem goes far beyond its visible and mandated activities. This is because it has 'bequeathed' to the Eurosystem an institutional framework which is at once a sound basis for a stability-oriented monetary policy and a generator of confidence in the fledgling European currency. Key elements of the Bundesbank's structure and ethos were transferred to the Eurosystem, in some cases in an even stricter form.

- The primary objective of monetary policy for the eurozone countries is to safeguard price stability; economic policy may be supported only if price stability is not put at risk.
- Monetary policy-makers are independent of instructions from national governments.
- Interest rate decisions take account of monetary growth because, in the longer term, the money stock and potential output have to develop at more or less the same pace if prices are to remain stable.
- Like the former Central Bank Council of the Deutsche Bundesbank, the supreme decision-making body of the Eurosystem has a relatively decentralized structure: the members of the Executive Board of the ECB and the presidents or governors of the national central banks of the eurozone countries have voting rights on the Governing Council of the European Central Bank.

These principles were transferred to the European Monetary Union because they were seen to be the source of the Bundesbank's success in maintaining price stability.

Currency stability needs central bank independence

'To safeguard the currency' – that was the statutory mandate conferred on the Bundesbank in 1957. The Bundesbank understood its primary objective as safeguarding price stability. This was very much the same thinking as at the Bank Deutscher Länder, the Bundesbank's forerunner institution, which was established in 1948. The success of the German central bank in maintaining stability was quite impressive: between 1948 and 1998, the average annual loss in the purchasing power of the Deutschmark was 2.8 per cent; following the low rates of inflation in the 1950s, there were few years in which the Bundesbank failed in its aim of not overstepping an annual inflation rate of 2 per cent, the rate which it deemed to be consistent with price stability. The loss of purchasing power in Germany was therefore still substantially smaller than in most other industrialized countries, which meant that, by comparison, the Deutschmark was exceptionally stable. That was another reason why it became the second most important reserve and investment currency in the world. It became the anchor currency in the European Monetary System which was established in 1979, and the central banks in Germany's partner countries increasingly endeavoured to reduce inflation differentials with the Deutschmark in order to prevent depreciations of their own currencies.

Two factors were crucial in achieving the comparatively large measure of stability: in its monetary policy, the Bundesbank generally gave clear priority to price stability over other economic policy objectives, such as stabilizing the economic cycle or exchange rates, unless other underlying conditions, such as its membership of fixed exchange rate systems, compelled it to purchase foreign currencies or to introduce low interest rates. Furthermore, the Bundesbank rarely lost sight of its medium-term objectives for achieving an appropriate rate of monetary growth. Whenever excessive inflation rates threatened, it checked the rise with higher interest rates.

However much the central bank and the federal government have invariably been concerned to act by mutual agreement, most of the Bundesbank's monetary policy stability measures have illustrated how important it has been for the German central bank to be independent of instructions from the federal government, an institutional arrangement which was desired politically and which is enshrined in law. The reason for this is that, time and again, federal governments have pressed for lower interest rates, i.e. an easing of monetary policy, in order to strengthen the economy although that would have given rise to inflation risks in the medium term. The Bundesbank and its forerunner, the Bank Deutscher Länder, would hardly have been able to cope with these conflicts without legal independence; the credibility of their commitment to stability would have become less credible, and greater inflationary expectations, for example on the part of management and trade unions, could have been reinforced and prices could have risen faster.

The Bundesbank's legacy: an example to be followed

The transfer of the Bundesbank's regulatory stability framework to the Eurosystem has nevertheless also encountered some criticism. Time and again, there have been doubts, for example, about the importance of monetary growth or the broadly based study of monetary and credit aggregates (monetary analysis) for monetary policy. It has been said that, in the eurozone, no monetary aggregate can be found that shows a consistent relationship with price developments and can therefore be used for monetary policy purposes. It has also been argued that the Bundesbank has not used the money stock as the crucial reference variable for its interest rate policy decisions. Recent studies have shown that this has indeed been very much the case in the medium term.

A stability-oriented monetary policy, such as the one that the Bundesbank has traditionally promoted and pursued, has not only been a bone of contention but has also frequently been criticized in principle. The primary objective of price stability and the allegedly undemocratic independence of the central bank from government instructions have quickly become targets for criticism. Not only are cyclical slumps said to be due to these two factors; it is also claimed that the weakness of growth and employment in Germany over a number of decades is also attributable to them. It is alleged, for example, that the high real interest rates arising from low inflation rates have greatly impeded investment.

It is true that the reduction in what, by German standards, were high inflation rates, was often linked in the short term with a relatively sharp fall in growth and employment. It is also true, however, that this was the price to be paid for the underpinning of longer-term economic prosperity and one that was worth paying. The stability of the Deutschmark protected savers and persons on fixed incomes against a massive fall in the value of money. And recent international studies confirm that monetary policy serves the real economy best when it stabilizes inflation expectations at a low level. The Bundesbank succeeded in doing just that in the medium term and gained the reputation of being a resolute 'inflation fighter' among market players and economic agents. The lower growth rates in Germany over the past thirty years and the constantly high level of unemployment were not the result of the Bundesbank's excessively rigid monetary policy but were, instead, the result of structural weaknesses in the German economy; investment suffered less from real interest rates that were too high and more from returns from fixed assets that were too low.

The Bundesbank's legacy of stability has so far proved to be effective in the European Monetary Union, too. Contrary to some fears that were expressed, the purchasing power of the euro is just as stable as that of the Deutschmark. As a matter of fact, the euro is very much like the Deutschmark. It is very much the Deutschmark that was taken over by the euro, but to be acceptable to the rest of Europe, it has deliberately chosen to take a different form. This is simply a matter of packaging the message to make it acceptable.

In sum, through its structure and institutional independence and through its goals and policies, the Deutsche Bundesbank can truly be said to be one of the greatest central banks in the world. Emerging economies should learn from this unique experience of success and achievement in central banking.

Notes

2 Central Bank Independence and Accountability: a Trade-off

1. This being said, defending the country's national sovereignty is a priority that takes precedence over the limited scope of central bank independence.
2. While many people would like to claim that the Central Bank of West African States (BCEAO) and the Bank of Central African States (BEAC) are the world's first supranational central banks, their dependency on the French Treasury takes away from them in some degree the features of truly independent central banks. While independence is often defined in relationship to the concerned governments, it is also important that central banks enjoy full independence versus foreign governments and international organizations. In the economic research conducted by several economists, this critical aspect is often overlooked.
3. The subprime mortgage financial crisis of 2007 was a sharp rise in home foreclosures which started in the United States during the autumn of 2006 and became a global financial crisis within a year. Subprime lending is a fancy financial term for high-interest loans to people who would otherwise be considered too risky for a conventional loan. These include middle-class families who have accumulated too much debt and low-income working families who want to buy a home in the inflated housing market. To cover their risk, lenders charge such borrowers higher-than-conventional interest rates. Or they make 'adjustable rate' loans, which offer low initial interest rates that jump sharply after a few years. Only a decade ago, subprime loans were rare. But starting in the mid-1990s, subprime lending began surging while Alan Greenspan (not Ben Bernanke) was Chairman of the Board of Governors of the Federal Reserve System; these loans comprised 8.6 per cent of all mortgages in 2001, soaring to 20.1 per cent by 2006. Since 2004, more than 90 per cent of the subprime mortgages came with exploding adjustable rates.

   With interest rates low, housing prices on a steady rise, and practically no government regulation, mortgage finance companies devised high-interest, high-fee schemes to entice families to take out loans that traditional savings banks would not make. Many of the lenders were legitimate operations providing a market for credit-risky people. But also there were huge corporations, such as Household Finance, that sought extraordinary profits through unsavoury means, called predatory loans. Not subject to government regulation, they bent the rules, lowering normal banking standards.

   Mortgage brokers, the street hustlers of the lending world, often used mail solicitations and ads that shouted, 'Bad Credit? No Problem!' 'Zero Percent Down Payment!' to find people who were closed out of home ownership, or homeowners who could be talked into refinancing. They seduced millions of people into signing on the dotted line. Although subprime lending has been concentrated in minority and low-income urban areas, it has spread to the middle-class suburbs. The subprime lenders did not hold on to these loans. Instead, they sold them – and the risk – to investment banks and investors who considered these high interest rate, subprime loans a goldmine. By 2007, the subprime business had become a $1.5 trillion global market for investors seeking high returns.

The whole scheme worked as long as borrowers made their monthly mortgage payments. When borrowers couldn't or wouldn't keep up the payments on these high-interest loans, what looked like a bonanza for everyone turned into a national foreclosure crisis and an international credit crisis. For millions of families, the American Dream of home ownership has become a nightmare. The mortgage meltdown has serious ripple effects. Foreclosed houses become vacant, deteriorate into eyesores, and detract from the neatness and feeling of well-being in neighbourhoods. Vacant houses also attract crime and make it more difficult for neighbours to purchase homeowner insurance. In neighbourhoods with several foreclosed homes, property values, and thus local property-tax revenues, plummet, making it harder for cities to provide good schools, police protection, and other services.

4. See Bob Woodward (2000).
5. All the speeches by the central bank staff and MPC members must be cleared by the governor to ensure consistency in the message to be transmitted to the public.

4 Building a Credible Central Bank in an Emerging Democracy

1. The principal mechanisms of the CFA franc zone are very complex, and carefully drafted to tie the economies of West and Central African countries to France. The CFA franc region represents a state-controlled zone of cooperation with the levers of control based in Paris. The African states that are members of this zone are dispersed in West and Central Africa. The principles of monetary cooperation between France and the member states of the CFA zone were formulated in the 1960s in a colonial pact which was reviewed in the monetary cooperation convention of 23 November 1972 between the member states of the Banque des Etats de l'Afrique Centrale (BEAC) (Bank of Central African States) and the French Republic on the one hand, as well as in the cooperation agreement of 4 December 1973 between the member states of the Union Economique et Monétaire Ouest Africaine (UEMOA) (or the West African Economic and Monetary Union) and the French Republic on the other hand. Just before France conceded to African demands for independence in the 1960s, it carefully organized its former colonies into a system of compulsory solidarity which consisted of obliging the African states to put 65 per cent of their foreign currency reserves into the French Treasury to guarantee the convertibility, at a rigid exchange rate of the CFA – a currency France had created for them. Today, while the CFA zone has achieved much in terms of economic integration and price stability, it is often criticized for failing to promote economic growth because the levers of policy intervention remain out of the control of the African policy-makers concerned. The biggest advantage that CFA countries have enjoyed comes from the very fact that the BEAC and the BCEAO are independent from African governments' political interference, particularly in the area of monetary policy and the financing of fiscal deficits. It is precisely this discipline that many other countries outside the CFA zone

have lacked, leading to uncontrolled currency printing, high inflation and monetary erosion.

5 A Strategic Vision for the Financial Sector

1. While the country has not completely stabilized its currency, I believe that deposit insurance premiums paid by financial institutions should be in foreign currency and reserves held in foreign currency. Once the national currency has become more stable and credible, it would be mandatory to convert the foreign currency premiums and reserves into local currency, except for investment diversification purposes.

6 A Strategic Agenda for the Currency

1. This coefficient is based on exchange rates prevailing in December 2007. It may change significantly when the reform takes place based on the exchange rate between the American dollar and the Congolese franc.

7 Leadership in Managing Changes in Central Banks

1. Ben S. Bernanke was sworn in on 1 February as Chairman and a member of the Board of Governors of the Federal Reserve System. Dr Bernanke also serves as Chairman of the Federal Open Market Committee, the System's principal monetary policy-making body. He was appointed as a member of the board to a full fourteen-year term, which expires on 31 January 2020, and to a four-year term as Chairman, which expires on 31 January 2010. Before his appointment as Chairman, Dr Bernanke was Chairman of the President's Council of Economic Advisers, from June 2005 to January 2006. Dr Bernanke has already served the Federal Reserve System in several roles. He was a member of the Board of Governors of the Federal Reserve System from 2002 to 2005; a visiting scholar at the Federal Reserve Banks of Philadelphia (1987–9), Boston (1989–90), and New York (1990–1, 1994–6); and a member of the Academic Advisory Panel at the Federal Reserve Bank of New York (1990–2002).

   Writing in the *New York Times Magazine* on Sunday, 20 January 2008, Roger Lowenstein profiled the Federal Reserve Chairman Ben Bernanke, finding him 'unable to re-instill a sense of confidence'. In Lowenstein's assessment, Bernanke failed to have the leadership to connect housing foreclosure with its ultimate effects. 'Perhaps worst of all,' Lowenstein continues, 'he has failed to persuade investors that the Federal Reserve, which was formed in 1913 for the very purpose of halting market panics, is up to the job.'

   Two days after the *New York Times Magazine* profile of Ben Bernanke was published, the financial markets were in panic all over the world, fearing that the US economy was heading into recession. To avert the deepening of the crisis in the financial market that saw the Dow Jones Industrial Average lose almost 1,000 points over the previous three months of 2007, the FOMC voted 8 to 1 on 22 January 2008 in an emergency meeting to cut the benchmark interest rate by 75 basis points from 5.25 to 3.5 per cent, citing a deepening of the housing contraction and a tightening of credit among the reasons for the move. Citing inflationary threats, European central banks did not follow the Fed's lead in cutting the rates, something that the market interpreted as lack of coordination among the world's largest central banks, or a clear challenge to the leadership of the US central bank.

There are two key points to keep in mind over this cut in interest rates by the Fed. The first is that the cut was surprisingly big. The second is that amidst the market noise and the paucity of positive economic news, the FOMC moved aggressively in advance of its pre-scheduled meeting, set for the week after 22 January 2008. The interest cut and the accompanying announcement were instrumental in averting a complete market crunch as the Dow, which opened 326 points down, recovered all the losses to close at about 298 points up on 22 January 2008. The Fed Chairman's credibility and leadership remained under scrutiny since the public believes that he should have been able to foresee the landscape of the housing crisis. David Rosenberg, chief North American economist for Merrill Lynch, is quoted in the *New York Times Magazine* saying that Bernanke is 'seriously behind the curve'. The performance and credibility of a central bank hinge very strongly on the leadership of its chairman. Such leadership is visible particularly during times of crisis. While critics suggest that he acted in panic in reaction to swings in the stock market in Europe and Asia, Ben Bernanke should be commended for taking the unusual step, although very late, of cutting the benchmark interest rate by 75 to prevent turmoil in the US financial market on 22 January 2008 and at the same to create the conditions for jump-starting the sluggish economy and avoiding a recession. However, it is my opinion that, notwithstanding this decisive cut, the swing in the US financial market could have become out of control and could have worsened the already sluggish economic prospects.

2. Roger Lowenstein, 'The Education of Ben Bernanke', *New York Times Magazine*, 20 January 2008.
3. Ibid.

Conclusion

1. Paul Volcker, 'Central Banks: Independent, Accountable, Linked', *International Herald Tribune*, 4 January 1994.

Bibliography

Bade, R. and Parkin, M. (1988) 'Central Bank Laws and Monetary Policy', Working Paper, Department of Economics at University of Western Ontario, October.

Baltensperger, E. and Dermine J. (1986) 'The Role of Public Policy in Financial Stability: a Cross Country Perspective', Working Paper No. 86/33, INSEAD, France.

Baltensperger, Ernst, Fischer, Andreas M. and Jordan, Thomas (2006) 'Strong Goal Independence and Inflation Targets', CEPR Discussion Paper No. 5915, November.

Barro, Robert J. (2003) *Nothing is Sacred: Economic Ideas for the New Millennium*, Cambridge, MA: MIT Press.

Barro, Robert J. and Gordon, David B. (1983) 'Rules, Discretion and Reputation in a Model of Monetary Policy', *Journal of Monetary Economics*, vol. 12, no. 1, July.

Blackman, Courtney N. (1982) *The Practice of Persuasion*, Bridgetown, Barbados: Cedar Press.

Blackman, Courtney N. (1988) *Central Banking in Theory and Practice: a Small State Perspective*, Caribbean Center for Monetary Studies, University of the West Indies, Trinidad and Tobago.

Blackman, Courtney N. (2006) *The Practice of Economic Management*, Kingston, Miami: Ian Randle Publishers.

Block, Peter (1987) *The Empowered Manager: Positive Political Skills at Work*, San Francisco: Jossey-Bass.

Block, Peter (1996) *Stewardship: Choosing Service over Self-Interest*, San Francisco: Berrett-Koehler Publishers.

Briault, Clive, Haldane, Andrew and King, Mervyn (1996) 'Independence and Accountability', Working Paper Series No. 49, Bank of England, April.

Brimmer, Andrew F. (1989) 'Politics and Monetary Policy: Presidential Efforts to Control the Fed', speech before the 75th Anniversary Luncheon, Board of Governors of the Federal Reserve System, Washington, D.C., 21 November.

Canuel, Olivier (2007) *Le système bancaire de la République Démocratique du Congo*, Ambassade de France en République Démocratique du Congo, Kinshasa, July.

Cukierman, Alex (1992) *Central Bank Strategy, Credibility and Independence: Theory and Evidence*, Cambridge, MA: MIT Press.

Debelle, G. and Fischer, S. (1994) 'How Independent Should a Central Bank Be?' Mimeo, MIT.

Demirguc-Kunt, A. and Kane, Edward J. (2002) 'Deposit Insurance Around the Globe: Where Does it Work?', *Journal of Economic Perspectives*, vol. 16, no. 2.

DePree, Max (1993) *Leadership Jazz*, New York: Currency Publishers.

DePree, Max et al. (1990) *Leadership is an Art*, New York: Currency Publishers.

Drucker, Peter F. (1993a) *The Effective Executive*, New York: HarperCollins.

Drucker, Peter F. (1993b) *Innovation and Entrepreneurship: Practice and Principles*, New York: HarperCollins.

Federal Deposit Insurance Corporation (2000) *International Directory of Deposit Insurers*, Washington, D.C.

Fischer, Stanley (1982) 'Seignorage and the Case for a National Money', *Journal of Political Economy*, vol. 90, no. 2, April.

Fischer, Stanley (1995) 'Modern Approaches to Central Banking', Working Paper No. 5064, National Bureau of Economic Research.

FresFalex, Maria L. (1991) 'Deposit Insurance Schemes: Their Nature, Role and Issues', The South East Asian Central Banks Research and Training Centre, Kuala Lumpur.

Friedman, Milton (1968) 'The Role of Monetary Policy', *American Economic Review*, vol. 58, no. 1.

Garcia, G. G. H. (1998) 'Deposit Insurance Around the World: Actual and Best Practices in 1998', paper presented to the FDIC International Conference on Deposit Insurance, Washington, D.C.

Green, Edward J. (2003) 'What Tasks Should Central Banks be Asked to Perform?' paper prepared for the Workshop on Central Bank Efficiency, Sveriges Riksbank, Stockholm, Sweden, May.

Greider, William (1989) *Secrets of the Temple: How the Fed Runs the Country*, New York: Touchstone.

Grier, Kevin (1987) 'Presidential Elections and Fed Policy: an Empirical Test', *Southern Economics Journal*, vol. 54, no. 2, October.

Grilli, Vittorio, Masciandro, Donato and Tabellini, Guido (1991) 'Political and Monetary Institutions and Public Financial Policies in the Industrial Countries', *Economic Policy: a European Forum*, vol. 6, no. 2, October.

Havrilesky, Thomas M. (1993) *The Pressures on Monetary Policy*, Boston, MA: Kluwer Academic Publishers.

Journal Officiel de la République Démocratique du Congo, 43ème année, Numéro Spécial, Kinshasa, May 2002.

Journal Officiel de la République Démocratique du Congo, Numéro Spécial (22762) de mai 2002: 'La loi 005/2002 du 07 mai 2002 relative à la constitution, à l'organisation et au fonctionnement de la Banque Centrale du Congo'.

Kabuya, K. and Kikassa, M. (eds) (1980) *Stabilisation économique et financière au Zaïre: De dévaluations en cascade à la démonétisation*, Kinshasa: Cepas.

Keynes, John Maynard (1935) *The General Theory of Employment, Interest, and Money*, New York: Harcourt, Brace and World.

Kikassa, M. (1980) *Les réformes monétaires au Zaïre de 1960 à 1979*, Kinshasa: Cepas.

Kouzes, James M. and Poser, Barry Z. (1995) *Credibility: How Leaders Gain and Lose It, Why People Demand It*, San Francisco: Jossey-Bass.

Kuediasala, Faustin (2006) 'Supplément de 5 milliards F de déficit dans le compte du trésor', *Le Potentiel*, Supplément, Kinshasa, 15 August.

Kydland, Finn E. and Prescott, Edward C. (1977) 'Rules Rather than Discretion: the Inconsistency of Optimal Plans', *Journal of Political Economy*, June.

Laeven, Luc (2004) 'The Political Economy of Deposit Insurance', World Bank Policy Research Working Paper No. 3247, Washington, D.C.

Lohman, Susanne (1992) 'Optimal Commitment in Monetary Policy: Credibility vs. Flexibility', *American Economic Review*, vol. 82, no. 1, March.

Lowenstein, Roger (2008) 'The Education of Ben Bernanke', *New York Times Magazine*, 20 January.

Luwansangu, Paul (2005) 'Stabilisation contre productive du franc congolais', *Le Potentiel*, Supplément, Kinshasa, 21 June.

Malingumu, Crispin (2005) 'Quelle politique de taux d'intérêts pour la Banque centrale du Congo?', *Le Potentiel*, Supplément, Kinshasa, 6 September.

Malingumu, Crispin (2006) 'Politique monétaire crédible', *Le Potentiel*, Supplément, Kinshasa, 11 July.

Melzer, T. (1996) 'Price Stability: an Attainable Goal for Monetary Policy', speech before the Missouri Valley Economic Association, March.

Minutes of the Board of Governors of the Federal Reserve System, 1965 to 2007, Washington, D.C.

Minutes of the Federal Open Market Committee of the Federal Reserve System, 1996 to 2006, Washington, D.C.

Monetary Policy Objectives: A Summary Report of the Federal Reserve Board, from 1996 to 2007, Washington, D.C.

Nordhaus, William D. (1975) 'The Political Business Cycle', *Review of Economic Studies*, vol. 42, no. 2, April.

Pollard, Patricia S. (2003) *A Look Inside Two Central Banks: the European Central Bank and the Federal Reserve*, Federal Reserve Bank of St. Louis, January/February.

Quinn, Robert E. (1996) *Deep Change: Discovering the Leader Within*, San Francisco: Jossey-Bass.

Reylandt, B. (1970) *L'inflation en pays sous-développés: Origines, mécanismes de propagation et effets des pressions inflationnistes au Congo, 1960–1969; interactions entre phénomènes monétaires et réels*, La Haye: Mouton.

Rogoff, Kenneth (1985) 'The Optimal Degree of Commitment to an Intermediate Monetary Target', *Quarterly Journal of Economics*, November.

Savage, G. T., Nix, T. W., Whitehead, C. J. and Blair, J. D. (1991) 'Strategies for Assessing and Managing Organizational Stakeholders', Academy of Management Executive, May.

Schwartz, Anna J. (1997) 'Central Banking in a Democracy', Western Economic Association, July.

Senge, Peter (1994) *The Fifth Discipline: the Art and Practice of a Learning Organization*, New York: Currency/Doubleday.

Swiss National Bank (1998) 'Monetary Policy of the Swiss National Bank'.

Tenreyro, Silvana and Olivei, Giovanni (2007) 'The Timing of Monetary Policy Shocks', *American Economic Review*, vol. 97, no. 3, June.

Tshiani, Noel K. (2000) 'L'indépendance des banques centrales, obligation de rendre compte, et incidence sur la politique monétaire: application à la République Démocratique du Congo', Université de Paris IX, Dauphine, Paris, February.

Tshiani, Noel K. (2001) 'Pour l'indépendance de la Banque Centrale du Congo', *Africa International*, 342, Paris, April.

Tshiani, Noel K. (2008) *Vision pour une monnaie forte: plaidoyer pour une nouvelle politique monetaire au Congo*, Paris: L'Harmattan.

Tshiunza, M. and Kabuya, K. (1978) 'L'expérience zaïroise en matière de taux de change', *Cahiers Economiques et Sociaux*, vol.16, no.1, March.

Tufte, Edward (1978) *Political Control of the Economy*, Princeton, NJ: Princeton University Press.

Volcker, Paul (1994) 'Central Banks: Independent, Accountable, Linked', *International Herald Tribune*, 4 January.

Walsh, Carl (1995) 'Optimal Contracts for Central Bankers', *American Economic Review*, vol. 85, no. 1, March.

White, Lawrence H. (2001) 'In What Respects Will the Information Age Make Central Banks Obsolete', *Cato Journal*, vol. 21, no. 2.

Woodward, Bob (2000) *Maestro-Greenspan's Fed and the American Boom*, New York: Simon & Schuster.

Index